I0068123

100 Tips for Creating a Champagne
Retirement on a Shoestring Budget

# 100 Tips for Creating a Champagne Retirement on a Shoestring Budget

Stewart H. Welch III
and
Associates at
The Welch Group, LLC
Welch Investments, LLC

**Limit of Liability / Disclaimer of Warranty:**

While the publisher and the author(s) have used their best efforts in preparing this book, they make no representations or warranties with respect to the accuracy or completeness of the contents of this book and specifically disclaim any implied warranties of merchantability or fitness for a particular purpose. The advice, tips, and strategies contained herein may not be suitable for your situation. You should consult with a professional where appropriate. Neither the publisher nor the author shall be liable for any loss of profit or any other damages, including but not limited to special, incidental, consequential, or other damages.

All rights reserved. No portion of this book may be reproduced, store in a retrieval system, or transmitted in any form or by any means—electronic, mechanical, photocopy, recording, scanning, or other—except for brief quotations in critical reviews or articles, without the prior written permission of the publisher.

Copyright © 2017 Stewart H. Welch III
All rights reserved.

ISBN-13: 9780692876183
ISBN-10: 0692876189
Library of Congress Control Number: 2017905615
The Welch Group, LLC, Birmingham, AL

All of the proceeds generated from the sale of this book will go directly to The Welch Group Foundation to further its stated mission.

## The Welch Group Foundation

Vision:
The Welch Group Foundation believes a single person can create positive ripple effects in his or her community. The foundation will strive to positively impact lives in the community by supporting organizations that will equip individuals to achieve this mission.

Mission:
The Welch Group Foundation exists to influence people's lives in a truly meaningful way by providing opportunities for advancement in education, skills for success in relationships and business, responsible financial guidance, and overall well-being.

## About The Welch Group and Welch Investments:

The Welch Group was founded in 1984 as a way for Stewart H. Welch III to serve the needs of the Birmingham, Alabama, community. As he assisted his clients in ensuring their financial future, he saw the need and importance for impartial financial advice from a trusted authority. The Welch Group was one of the first firms in the country to provide fee-only investment management and financial planning services for clients and now serves client families throughout the United States.

Welch Investments was founded in 1999 by Stewart H. Welch III. His vision was to create a fee-only financial planning and advisory firm with *no* minimum-asset requirement so that people who traditionally did not have access an impartial, fee-only financial advisor would now be able to do so.

Today, the combined companies work with families all over the United States and manage over $1 billion in assets.

# Table of Contents

# INTRODUCTION

You've all heard the phrase, "If you fail to plan, you plan to fail." This is true in most aspects of one's life, but it's particularly true as it pertains to retirement planning. Nowadays, more times than not, the only option available to workers and their spouses for retirement savings are defined-contribution plans (401(k)s, 403(b)s, etc.), in which the funding responsibility lies entirely with the individual instead of his or her employer. Unfortunately, this has left many people facing an underfunded (and unfulfilling) retirement. Research shows that the average American between the ages of fifty-five and sixty-four has about $104,000 in retirement savings. That would translate to a lifetime annuity payment of about $300 per month. Hmmm. Even when you add Social Security, that amounts to a pretty dismal retirement income. As a result, many have to either delay retirement or lower their standard of living far beyond their preference during retirement in order to supplement for their inadequate funding.

Obviously, to avoid this would mean to successfully plan and execute a retirement plan. While every individual has different needs and desires that dictate his or her retirement goals, proper and sufficient levels of savings before and during retirement are central to every plan. No matter who you are, what stage of life you're in, or what your income is, a satisfactory retirement begins with savings—and everybody has different ways of generating and managing his or her savings. The alternative to saving enough money for retirement is to find creative ways to live better on less money.

To that end, I invited each person in our office to share a few of his or her personal tips as they pertain to generating and managing savings, as well as ideas for living better through creative expense management. This book is a compilation of each tip we received—some short and some long. Coincidentally, the following one hundred tips range a great deal in terms of variation and scope. While the book's contributors all share certain commonalities such as working in the same office, each person is different, which translated into the incredible breadth of content we received. Each contributor represents a different background, education level, work experience, and career stage. With that in mind, no matter who you happen to be, there will assuredly be content presented that not only will peak your interest, but it will also be entirely applicable to your everyday life.

# TRANSPORTATION

**Tip #1: Buying a Car**

If you are financing the purchase of a vehicle, don't define its affordability by your capacity to make monthly payments. We spend hundreds of thousands of dollars on vehicle purchases over the course of a lifetime, often without giving it much thought. Many of us shop for a car based on what we want, limited by the affordability of a monthly payment. The result is an unending pattern of buying more car than we can truly afford while paying interest charges forever.

A better idea: Instead, evaluate a vehicle purchase within the context of your overall financial life. Will you be able to make steady progress toward retirement and other savings goals, such as a down payment toward a home purchase, if you buy the vehicle under consideration? If you can become clear about your goals, you will have firmer footing for making a vehicle-purchase decision. Don't get trapped into mindlessly buying vehicles with eternal monthly payment obligations while undermining other goals. Instead, make purposeful vehicle-purchase decisions, fully aware of the total cost of the vehicle and its impact on the achievement of other goals that are important to you.

*Contributor: Woodard Peay, CFP®*

## Tip #2: Used vs. New Car

Can you have the car of your dreams even if you don't have a lot of cash? Absolutely! A friend of mine owned a high-end Range Rover, and one day I rode with him and really liked the car. Now, this is an expensive car, which he bought new for $100,000. He also happened to like to trade cars often, so I kept checking in with him until he was ready to sell. By that time the Kelly Blue Book value was $45,000, which is what I paid him for a car I love that had only thirty-six thousand miles. OK, I know $45,000 is a lot of money, but the point is that you can do the same thing with the car of your dreams:

- Step 1. Decide on the car of your dreams.
- Step 2. Ask yourself whether anyone you know owns the car you want.
- Step 3. Let the person know of your desire to purchase the car when he or she is ready to sell,

and keep in touch. Every few months, I'd remind my friend that I had dibs on his car. He'd laugh and say, "Great!" When he got ready to sell, I was the first person he thought of.

- Step 4. Research to ensure that the agreed-upon price of the deal is relatively close to fair market value as determined by a reliable source such as Kelly Blue Book.

*Contributor: Stewart Welch III, AEP, CFP®*

## Tip #3: Financing—Breaking the Cycle of Interest Payments

If you can't pay cash, what's your best financing strategy?

What is the most often asked question of a car salesperson? "How much are my payments?" This is the wrong question being asked, and moreover, it is being asked to the wrong person! Car people have been asked this question so many times for so long that they got smart and decided if they extended the term over which payments are made, they could sell much more expensive cars. Now they offer payment terms of sixty months or more. Don't fall for this trap! You decide how much payment you can afford over no longer than twenty-four months, and let that guide your decision on how much car you can afford to buy. Almost certainly a used car will make more sense than a new car. Now—and here's the key—once you've paid off your car, continue to make payments into a "new car fund," and continue to save until you have the cash for your next car. Note that you'll always continue this car savings plan. Maybe periodically increase your investment as you save for your dream car!

*Contributor: Stewart Welch III, AEP, CFP®*

## Tip #4: Utilize Research Tools before Purchasing

Kelly Blue Book: A website that tracks car and truck values according to actual sales by region. Use this site to get a good estimate of the value of a car you are considering purchasing (or of your own car if you're thinking of selling). Visit the site at www.kbb.com.

*Contributor: Stewart Welch III, AEP, CFP®*

## Tip #5: Buy a Used Car under Warranty

Most new cars depreciate (drop in value) about 20 percent or more as soon as you drive them off the lot. By buying used, you'll instantly save 20 percent or more. With a used car, people worry most about inheriting someone else's problems. However, if you buy a used car that is still under warranty, you get two benefits:

1. Any problems you have will be fixed at no cost to you during the warranty period.

2. Typically, you can review all the warranty work done on the car before you purchase it. Just have the seller give the dealer permission to release all repair/warranty work paperwork. If there's an unusual amount of work, this car might be a lemon that you'll want to avoid.

*Contributor: Stewart Welch III, AEP, CFP®*

## Tip #6: What to Do before You Purchase a Car That Is out of Warranty

If you are buying a car that is out of warranty, you'll want to do two things before you buy:

1. Get the seller to give their repair shop permission to allow you to review all repair records. Then you should review the records looking to two things. First, are there any repairs of a major significance, such as a blown head gasket or a bad transmission, that would suggest you to skip this car? Do the repairs show that the car was brought in for regular maintenance? You want to buy a car that the owner took pride in keeping up the maintenance.

2. Finally, as a last step before you buy a used car, have a mechanic whom you trust give the car a full inspection. Any deviations from the seller's description of the condition of the car can be used to negotiate a lower price.

*Contributor: Stewart Welch III, AEP, CFP®*

### Tip #7: Know If the Car Has Been Wrecked

A car that was involved in a significant wreck is worth less than a similar car that was never wrecked. Don't expect the seller to volunteer this information. First, ask him or her if the car was ever involved in a wreck. Then rely on the famous words from President Ronald Reagan, "Trust, but verify!" Spend a few bucks and get a history report from www.CarFacts.com. If the seller didn't tell you the truth, it's a sign that you better move on, or at a minimum, you should negotiate a lower price.

*Contributor: Stewart Welch III, AEP, CFP®*

### Tip #8: Save for Future Vehicle Purchases

In order to balance the cost of a vehicle purchase with other goals, buy a less expensive vehicle, operate it as long as it remains safe and reliable, and make periodic payments to a reserve fund in anticipation of your next vehicle purchase.

Your ultimate goal is to be in position to buy your next vehicle with cash or to at least be able to make a significant down payment. There are two benefits to you as you reduce the need to finance a vehicle purchase. First, avoidance of costly interest charges, which can significantly increase the total cost of your vehicle over its life. Second, if you pay cash for a vehicle rather than using credit, you are more mindful of its true cost and not as inclined to buy a more expensive vehicle based on the capacity to make a monthly payment.

*Contributor: Woodard Peay, CFP®*

## Tip #9: Maintain Your Vehicle

While regular tune-ups, oil changes, and other maintenance seems expensive, they can help extend the life of your vehicle significantly, resulting in longevity. Said longevity will help avoid premature purchases down the road, whether they be paying for an entirely new car or costly repairs.

*Contributor: Andrea Messick*

## Tip #10: Patience and Research Pay Off

When it comes to purchasing a vehicle, having the ability to efficiently research your options and remain patient goes a long way! I was recently able to save a substantial amount of money by purchasing a truck that I located on Craigslist. I had done all of the preliminary work far in advance; I knew what price I was willing to pay based on my budgetary constraints, and I knew just about exactly the type of truck I wanted based on extensive market research. I had identified several trucks that fit my pre-determined criteria at local car lots by conducting regularly Internet searches. However, I was resolute in my determination to not pay top dollar for a vehicle I knew I can buy for far less from an individual. After weeks of scouring Craigslist ads, I found a near-perfect match! I contacted the individual who had listed the truck and explained to him that I was very serious in my interest, but that any sale would be contingent upon my intense scrutiny. Of course, he was incredibly understanding (any reasonable seller would be). After test-driving the truck on numerous occasions, we agreed upon the terms of the sale. All in all, I was able to save roughly $7,000 off of the average retail price simply by taking my time and being meticulous in my search.

*Contributor: Brett Norris*

# HOUSING

## Tip #11: Renting vs. Owning

I used to be a firm believer in the American dream of owning a house. Not being a do-it-yourselfer, I purchased what I thought to be the perfect house that would need little work and was within my budget. Then the roof needed to be replaced, then dead branches needed to be cut out of trees, then other trees needed to be cut down, then plumbing work needed to be done to reduce water pressure, then significant drainage work in the back yard was needed, then another tree had to be cut down, and the list goes on and on.

Fortunately for the couple who bought my house, most of the necessary work had been done, but all of those issues caused me to lose a lot of sleep for the three years that I owned my home. Being a self-proclaimed finance nerd, I did a detailed analysis to see how my overall financial picture would look if I rented. Factoring in equity payments, tax deductibility of interest and property taxes, and adding back maintenance, I figured that I could actually pay several hundred dollars per month more for rent than my mortgage payment and be no worse off financially. Plus, I now have a landlord that handles any maintenance issues for me.

I do intend to buy again one day, but I will be much more careful with my next purchase. In the meantime, I am enjoying the reduced stress of no longer being a homeowner! Owning a house can be a great experience, but make sure you know what you are getting yourself into, and buy for the right reasons, not just because you think you are throwing money away by renting.

*Contributor: Foster Hyde, CFP®, CFA*

## Tip #12: Maximize Retirement Cash Flow Using a Reverse Mortgage

A Home Equity Conversion Mortgage (HECM), commonly referred to as a reverse mortgage, is essentially the opposite of a traditional mortgage. With a traditional mortgage, you borrow money from a lender, and you repay the loan in monthly installments until it is repaid (including interest). With a reverse mortgage, you're taking a loan on your home and, instead of you paying the lender, the lender pays you! You can receive a lump-sum, a line of credit, fixed monthly payments (ideal for retirement planning), or a combination of the three choices.

Here's a quick guide to using a reverse mortgage:

- You, and your co-owner if you have one, must be age sixty-two or older in order to qualify for a reverse mortgage. You must pay off any existing mortgages either before or as part of the transaction of acquiring a reverse mortgage.
- The amount of money you can get depends on several factors including your age, the value of your home, and the current mortgage interest rates. A good rule of thumb is 50 to 60 percent of your home's appraised value. A Federal Housing Administration (FHA) appraisal is required.
- Mortgage company takes 100 percent of the risks. This is one of the key benefits of a reverse mortgage. If, when you die or move out of the home, it is sold for less than the mortgage balance, neither you nor your heirs owe anything! Technically, you will pay the FHA Mutual Mortgage Insurance Fund a small premium, and they bear the risk!
- Unused equity remains with you or your heirs. At death, or when you choose to move out, any sale proceeds after satisfying the mortgage are yours (or your heirs').

- You make no payments. During the term of the reverse mortgage, you are not required to make any payments. You are required to maintain the home and pay property taxes and homeowners insurance.

- You have multiple choices for how you can take your money:

  1. <u>Monthly income for life</u>. If you choose to take your money in the form of a monthly income, the income will continue for as long as you remain in the home—even if that's a really long time!

     *Strategy*: Create a guaranteed income for you and your spouse for as long as you live in your home. We find that most people want to live in their home as long as possible.

  2. <u>Lump sum</u>. If you choose a lump sum, you are free to do whatever you choose with the money. There are no restrictions.

  3. <u>Line of Credit (LOC)</u>. If you choose a LOC, your money sits there waiting for you to draw on it. You only pay interest on the money you take out of your LOC.

  4. <u>Combination</u>. You can choose a combination of the plans above.

- Money coming from a reverse mortgage is not subject to income taxes and will not affect your Social Security.
- When you are no longer living in the home, the mortgage becomes due, but you're allowed ample time to sell. Once sold, the proceeds are used first to pay off the loan, and any remaining equity is returned to you or your heirs.
- Reverse mortgages are governed by the FHA, and therefore the credit and income qualifications are minimal. The FHA simply wants to be certain you can afford to pay homeowner's insurance premiums and property taxes.

**Example:** Couple, both age sixty-five with a home valued at $200,000 and no debt. They have no kids and currently are planning on leaving all of their assets to charity. Both have retired, so they are currently experiencing shrinking income but do not want to move out of their house. To help supplement their lost earnings, they take out a reverse mortgage, which provides them with an annuity payment as long as they live there. After both individuals pass away, the loan comes due and the bank sells the house and recoups the loan balance. The unused equity passes in accordance to their estate plan.

If you need more cash flow for your retirement and have a strong desire to stay in your home for as long as possible, the reverse mortgage is a strategy you should explore. As with any mortgage loan, you'll want to shop around for the best pricing.

*Contributor: Stewart Welch III, AEP, CFP®*

## Tip #13: Calculate Your Possibilities!

For a handy calculator to help you estimate your reverse mortgage loan possibilities, visit the Resource Center at www.WelchGroup.com; click on "Links" and then "Reverse Mortgage Loan Calculator."

*Contributor: Stewart Welch III, AEP, CFP®*

## TIP #14: Take Less in the Beginning

If, during the first twelve months, you are willing to take less than 60 percent of available funds, the FHA will eliminate much of the up-front mortgage insurance, which will significantly reduce your closing costs.

*Contributor: Stewart Welch III, AEP, CFP®*

## Tip #15: Share Home-Maintenance Tools

Consider splitting the cost of a high-priced home-maintenance tools that you rarely use. A few years ago, my husband had to spend hours in the yard every weekend to keep up with the endless barrage of leaves in our yard. With a newborn at home, time together as a family was precious. He really wanted a backpack leaf blower that would be more powerful and efficient because of the layout and size of our yard, but that wasn't in the budget. Ultimately, he and a friend in our neighborhood decided to share a nice blower. They split the cost and drastically reduced the amount of time spent working in the yard each weekend.

*Contributor: Beth Moody, CFP®*

## Tip #16: Avoid Capital Gains

Almost everyone knows about the tax benefits that come with home ownership such as the deductions for mortgage interest and property taxes. However, the break that has the potential to offer the most benefit often goes unmentioned—the capital gains exclusion when you sell your home. The exclusion allows for you to make up to $250,000 ($500,000 if you file a joint return with your spouse) on the sale of your home and not pay any capital gains tax. To qualify for the exclusion, there are two caveats to be aware of: the home you are selling had to have been your primary residence for at least two out of the last five years, and you had to have owned it during that period.

For example, if a couple purchased a home twenty-two months ago and sold it for a gain, their entire gain would be a taxable capital gain. If the couple had waited an additional two months until they sold it, they would have been able to exclude the entire gain and have no tax liability on the sale!

Practically speaking, this exclusion will likely come into play for individuals who have either owned their home for a long period (over which, housing prices have risen), or for people who have done renovations to their home that subsequently improved their home's value.

*Contributor: Brett Norris*

## Tip #17: Keep Up with Receipts (from Renovation Costs)

Obviously, any capital improvement to your home should theoretically improve its value correspondingly. That said, it's important to keep up with the costs associated with any improvement because they count toward your adjusted cost basis in your home, which can potentially play a big factor in how much tax you owe down the road.

For example, let's assume Jim has a home budget of $400,000. Instead of using all of his money on a brand-new house, he decides to buy a fixer-upper. He buys the home for $300,000 and then spends another $100,000 on renovations for an adjusted cost basis of $400,000. Several years later, Jim sells his house for $650,000, which means he has a capital gain of $250,000 ($650,000 sale price minus the $400,000 adjusted cost basis). Assuming he qualifies for capital gains exclusion on the sale of his residence, he owes no tax (he is single and gets an automatic $250,000 exclusion). If he had not kept up with his receipts for the $100,000 spent on improvements, his $100,000 adjustment to his cost basis would have been disallowed. This means that his cost basis would have been $300,000 and his reported gain on the sale would be $350,000, resulting in a capital gain of $100,000 (after the $250,000 exclusion).

*Contributor: Brett Norris*

## Tip #18: Do-It-Yourself Renovations

My husband and I have saved money on our kitchen update by being our own contractor. We worked with the cabinet company ourselves and hired the plumber, electrician, tile installer, and more on our own. We did the painting ourselves. The painting estimate was $4,000.00!

Moreover, we found someone who wanted our old cabinets, countertops, sink, and appliances. He is removing everything and taking it all away for free. This has saved us roughly $850.00. It is a win-win as he is happy to get the cabinets and appliances, and we are happy to get rid of them.

*Contributor: Ramona Boehm*

# INVESTING

## Tip #19: Your Asset Allocation Is the Number One Determinant of Your Investment Results

The term "asset allocation" refers to the relative proportions of stocks, bonds, and cash in your investment mix. Over a longer period of ten to twenty years, stocks generally return about twice as much as bonds. If you are ten years or more away from planned retirement, consider holding over one-half of your assets in stock mutual funds. Depending on the custodian for your retirement plan, there may well be over two hundred mutual funds offered as investment options. Employees often become overwhelmed by some many choices with no means for making a decision.

There are two possible ways to work around this issue. First, many retirement plans offer an all-in-one target-date fund that can be selected to coincide with your planned retirement date. These target-date funds are essentially funds comprised of other mutual funds. Over time, the target-date fund manager changes the mix of underlying investments so that you're holding more bonds and less stocks in recognition of your approaching retirement. As long as you are comfortable with the mix of stocks, bonds, and other investments held by the target-date fund over time, this is a great way to eliminate most of your own involvement in terms of picking funds and rebalancing over time. Before investing in a target-date fund, confirm that the internal expenses are 0.75 percent or lower.

Another option is to combine either a low-cost stock index fund such as the S&P 500, or a broadly diversified US large-company stock fund with a bond fund comprised of individual bonds with high credit ratings. A bond fund that relies heavily on US Treasuries, bonds issued by a government agency, or highly rated corporate bonds are examples of bond funds with high credit quality.

An allocation to bonds in your retirement account mix serves the important role of reducing the volatility of your portfolio. When stocks get caught in a significant downturn, bonds are more likely to hold their value. Any allocation to cash should be kept to a minimum since this asset class typically produces low returns. Your mission is to devise an asset allocation that affords the potential for sufficient growth to attain your retirement goal while reducing your exposure to stock-market volatility so that you don't panic out of the market during a big bear market. Striking a balance between stocks and bonds is the means by which you make this tradeoff.

*Contributor: Woodard Peay, CFP®*

## BONUS TIP: The Asset Allocation "Sweet Spot"

After thirty-plus years of observing the stock and bond markets, I've determined that the best trade-off of returns versus risks (the so-called sweet spot) is an allocation of 60 percent stocks and 40 percent bonds. In a bear market, the stock market drops because of heavy investor selling. As investors sell, they are raising cash and often that cash will be used to buy bonds (typically high-quality bonds such as treasury bonds). The money pouring into bonds causes bonds to rise, helping offset a portion of the falling stocks. In general, with this 60/40 allocation, we believe you'll receive approximately 80 percent of the stock-market return over time with less than one-half of the stock-market volatility.

*Contributor: Stewart Welch III, AEP, CFP®*

## Tip #20: Earn a 50 Percent Return in One Month—Guaranteed

Would you be wary of someone promising you a 50 percent return on a twelve-month investment? How about a *one month* investment? I assume (hope) your early-warning antennas are blaring in your head as well they should be. But there might be a way to actually make this happen for a number of really smart people. To determine if you are one of the lucky ones, take a moment to determine how much you have contributed to your company 401(k) plan as compared to the amount of company matching contribution. For example, let's assume your company matches fifty cents on the dollar up to 6 percent of your compensation (a typical company matching program). If your salary is $100,000, your company would provide matching funds on up to $6,000 of contributions for this calendar year ($3,000 match). If you're already having the company deduct $200 per month, you're on schedule to invest $2,400 this year (with matching contributions of another $1,200). But you're leaving $3,600 of potential unmatched contributions on the table.

Are you really interested in earning a 50 percent return in one month? If so, have your human-resources department up your 401(k) contribution by $3,600 from your December paycheck(s). Your $3,600 investment will yield a 50 percent return based on the $1,800 employer matching contribution! In many cases, you can increase your payroll deduction directly through your company's 401(k) website.

OK, I admit that I used a little bit of trickery to get you to think about the importance of fully capturing your company's matching contribution, but failing to do so is like turning your back on a portion of your compensation package—you're just leaving money on the table. And, for many people, it never occurs to them that they could significantly adjust their payroll deduction in the last month of the year.

## BONUS TIP: How to solve "I can't afford it!"

Another barrier I often hear is, "I need all of my paycheck to pay my bills!" Look for ways you can get a bit creative:

- Use personal savings. Use personal savings or money from a personal investment account to help cover your December bills.
- Use year-end bonus money. If you are expecting a year-end bonus, consider paying some of your December bills through whatever means necessary (savings, credit cards, etc.) to handle your cash-flow needs until your bonus comes in.

- Use a home equity line of credit (HELOC). If you are using a HELOC or other forms of debt, be sure you have a sure source of repayment such as a bonus, significant pay raise, savings, or investments.

Even if you're already investing enough in your 401(k) to capture your company's matching contribution, this is a strategy worth considering since you obviously will benefit from an income-tax deduction and long-term tax-deferred growth.

*Contributor: Stewart Welch III, AEP, CFP®*

## Tip #21: Don't Forget to Sweat the Big Stuff

All throughout my adolescence and early adulthood, I had been taught to cut back on the small things—to monitor any and all discretionary spending as a way to help finance an incredible savings fund that would theo-retically grow into an enormous nest egg by way of savvy investing and the powerful combination of compounding and time. This is all absolutely true. By my calculations, if you were to save twenty dollars each month and deposit it into an account in which you earned a relatively modest return of 6 percent annually, your hypothetical savings account would grow to an astounding $76,000 over the course of 50 years. This $20 savings could be generated by a plethora of small things such as cutting back on your habitual Starbucks trips, by ordering water at restaurants instead of tea or wine, or maybe by cancelling underutilized magazine and newspaper subscriptions.

Unfortunately, illustrations like this were usually where the advice ended for me when I was growing up. Admittedly, the prospect of having an additional $76,000 in retirement is nothing to scoff at, and the advice was sound, but I was amazed at what I found when I adjusted the one variable in this model that was easiest to manipulate—the amount of money I put back each month. I ran the same simulation in Excel again, except this time I assumed a $500 monthly savings. At 50 basis points per month, this yielded $1.9 million by year fifty—$1,913,081.34, to be exact. I was amazed. Determined to figure out where I could find $500 a month, I immediately started looking into my budget. Alas, I realized that I did not have an extra $500 to spare, nor did I spend that much on excessive or luxury items. I was also aware that many other young adults didn't either. After being discouraged at my inability to raise $500 each month, it suddenly it hit me: I had not been looking in all of the right places for savings. Places that many of us consider mandatory or static parts of our budget such as a mortgage, rent, or a car payment. Over time, these expenses become so entrenched in our brains that the monthly expense from our bank account becomes ingrained in our psyche as an inevitability. Even worse, each time that we receive a raise or experience a windfall, we unfailingly raise our standard of living to match, a phenomenon commonly referred to as "lifestyle creep." So instead of buying the most expensive house and car you can afford, I strongly urge you to consider maintaining your current standard of living when you receive a salary increase. By continuing to drive the same car for a few more years or live in the same house, you could begin to generate that aforementioned $500 each month. After that, simply sit back and allow compounding to go to work for you. Before you know it, you'll be closer to an adequately funded retirement than you ever imagined possible.

Beyond the empirical points of this exercise, it's likely that you would also develop the habit of saving at a young age if you were to follow this advice, which would pay off tenfold over your life.

*Contributor: Brett Norris*

## Tip #22: Avoid Holding a Concentrated Investment Position

As professional advisors, we recommend you limit your holdings of any single stock position to no more than 5 percent of your total portfolio. While there are few more exciting personal financial situations than to be the holder of a large stock position that is rapidly advancing, nothing is more devastating than to experience the demise of a concentrated position. Any company's stock can get into sell-off significantly, no matter how well established and well regarded the company may be.

Other than inheritance, by far the most frequent instance in which we encounter a concentrated investment holding is that of an employee's own company's publicly traded stock. Through participation in employee stock ownership plans (ESOPs), incentive stock options, company matching provisions that may include the company stock, and outright purchase of shares, long-term employees often accumulate large quantities of their company's stock over a career. I once worked with the head of an accounting department for the largest subsidiary of a Fortune 500 company. Over a work career spanning almost forty years, this accountant had amassed almost $1 million of this company's stock, along with much smaller positions of company stock in his retirement account. For many years during the accountant's work history, this company's stock had enjoyed outstanding returns and received high praise from Wall Street analysts.

Because the accountant was within a couple of years of retirement, I asked the accountant how he could be so comfortable holding his entire retirement account in this company's stock. After all, this represented a lifetime of hard work and diligent saving. He was quick to respond that he knew more about the details of the company than anyone, including the CEO. He was confident that he knew more than the analysts who followed this company. You have already guessed the remainder of the story; within a year's time, the share price for this company dropped from the mid $80s to around $7 per share! There was even a valid concern over the solvency of the corporation at one point. The accountant's expectations for a comfortable, well-deserved retirement were utterly destroyed in less than a year with no hope of recovery.

It is my suspicion that employees who accumulate concentrated positions in their company's stock do so for a host of reasons. Possibilities include loyalty to their employer and high familiarity with their company that seems to breed a false sense of perceived safety. The same person with a concentrated position in their company's stock would never consider buying a similar position in some other company under any circumstances. Within the confines of your retirement plan, you are generally free to sell most of your company's stock with no tax consequence, using the proceeds to invest in other areas to diversify and reduce your risk. Liquidation of your company's shares in an employee stock purchase plan or options requires consideration of tax consequences.

*Contributor: Woodard Peay, CFP®*

## Tip #23: Incrementally Increase Your Savings over Time

One of the best things you can do when starting out in the real world is to begin saving a percentage of your income. Most rules of thumb put this in the range of 10 to 15 percent. If you started out doing that, congratulations! However, if you're like most Americans, something got in the way of disciplined savings—either a true money mistake or something out of your control. There may be no way to get to the 15 percent savings benchmark in one year. If you're in this camp, I'd encourage you to set a goal to increase your savings by at least 1 percent every year. Below are three examples. All three involve Mike, a twenty-five-year-old just out of school. His starting salary is $30,000, and for the sake of simplicity, we'll assume this stays the same until retirement at age sixty-seven.

- <u>Example One:</u> Mike starts saving 15 percent of his $30,000 annual income immediately ($4,500/year). Mike invests this money and earns an annual return of 6 percent. At age sixty-seven, he will have accumulated over $800,000.

- Example Two: Mike has some other obligations and can only save 3 percent the first year he works ($900/year). Mike is determined to save more and commits to increasing his savings, so he'll save 4 percent of his income the next year ($1,200/year) and 5 percent the year after that ($1,500/year). He'll continue increasing his savings until he gets to 15 percent ($4,500/year), and he'll continue with the 15 percent until age sixty-seven. Mike invests this money and earns an annual return of 6 percent. At age sixty-seven, he will have accumulated close to $600,000.

- Example Three: Mike wants to save *something*, so he commits to saving 3 percent of his income ($900/year) but never increases his savings. He invests the money and earns an annual return of 6 percent. At age sixty-seven, he will have accumulated more than $160,000.

The main point of this tip is not to get discouraged if you can't start saving the maximum recommended amount immediately. Obviously, Mike's savings in example one produced the highest savings balance, but the small increases in example two have a huge impact compared to example three, when Mike doesn't make any changes.

*Contributor: Beth Moody, CFP®*

## BONUS TIP: How Much Should You Be Saving to Achieve Financial Freedom by Retirement?

Assuming you're just starting to save:

> In your twenties: 10 percent of gross income
> In your thirties: 15 percent of gross income
> In your forties: 20 to 25 percent of gross income
> In your fifties: OK, you have a big problem. You'll need to figure out how to substantially cut expenses (downsize your home; spouse get a job; you get a second income, etc.) and save as much money as possible.
> In your sixties: I hope you love what you do because you'll need to continue doing it as long as you live!

*Contributor: Stewart Welch III, AEP, CFP®*

## Tip #24: Decide If Dollar-Cost Averaging Is Right for You

For risk-averse investors, whose guiding principle is capital preservation, the notion of injecting a lump sum of cash into a volatile market can cause an incredible amount of unnecessary anxiety and stress. To help mitigate the potential of a sudden and sizable loss and the emotional instability that would accompany said risk, investors can choose a simple and effective strategy called "dollar-cost-averaging."

With dollar-cost-averaging, the investor consistently invests a fixed amount of money into the market at regular intervals over a predetermined period instead of investing an entire lump sum all at once. Doing this helps to eliminate the timing risk of inadvertently buying at the peak of a bull market.

For example, let's assume you have $10,000 of cash to invest, of which you plan to invest $2,500 each month over the next four months. The price at the end of month one was $100, month two was $89, month three was $92, and month four was $98. By dollar-cost-averaging into this hypothetical market, your average cost was $94.75, and you limited your exposure to the market downturn. Alternatively, if you had invested the entire lump sum at month one, your cost would have been $100 and you would have been entirely at risk for the sudden decline in price. Moreover, you were able to inject a portion of your cash into the market while it was at its trough of $89, thereafter capturing a piece of the rebound in price.

It's important to note that this strategy inherently requires the investor to leave some of their money in cash or cash equivalents for the period preceding the investment, not allowing them to participate in the market, which would be off-putting to risk-seeking investors. The potential of missing out on a market run-up has to be taken into account before committing to this strategy. (You would still experience a gain if you were dollar-cost averaging into a bull market, just not as much as if you had invested the entire lump sum all at once.)

*Contributor: Brett Norris*

## Tip #25: Achieve a Balance of Qualified and Nonqualified Assets before Retirement

Achieving a good balance between qualified (IRAs, 401(k)s, etc.) and nonqualified (after tax accounts) assets before retirement can allow you to manage your tax liability during retirement. Remember that in retirement there is no new cash flow coming in from your job, so the money has to come from somewhere for you to pay your bills and do the things you want to do. If all of your assets are held within qualified accounts (IRAs) then each dollar you take out of those accounts is getting taxed at ordinary income rates, which could potentially place you in a high tax bracket. If, however, you have additional assets in nonqualified accounts (personal investment accounts) you have the opportunity to keep your tax rates low by taking advantage of favorable capital gains and qualified dividend rates. Note: Seek the advice of your personal accountant and investment manager before determining if you are able to take advantage of this approach.

*Contributor: Marshall Clay, CFP®*

## BONUS TIP: Do a Trial Tax Return in January of each Year

In Marshall's Tip #25 above, we recommend doing a trial tax return in January of each year to determine a guesstimate of your income taxes for the year. As a retiree, assuming you have money in both personal investment accounts and retirement accounts, you get to decide which 'bucket' to draw cash flow from and how much. A few 'what-if' calculations will allow you to decide where to draw from to optimize your taxes both now and in the future. We have a client who had about half of his retirement money in each bucket, and for special reasons, our goal was to pay no income taxes. For the past ten-plus years, we've been able to achieve this goal by carefully analyzing where to draw his cash-flow funds from.

*Contributor: Stewart Welch III, AEP, CFP®*

## Tip #26: Rebalance Your Retirement-Plan Holdings

When you develop a target asset allocation for your retirement plan account, the weighting of stocks to bonds should represent a balance between potential return and associated risk. Because your stock and bond holdings will rarely experience the same returns over a significant period of time, it is necessary to sell a portion of the asset class that had a higher return and to use the proceeds to buy more of the lagging asset. By systematically rebalancing your retirement account at least annually, you are forced to sell high and to buy low. Without taking this action periodically, your original balance between your stocks and bonds will diverge from the original mix (goal). For example, if stocks outperformed bonds since your last periodic rebalancing, stocks are now over weighted. The result is that you are taking more risk than you may be prepared to endure during a bear market. By selling some of your stocks and buying more bonds, you not only capture a gain on the portion of stocks sold but also reduce your risk. Within a retirement plan, the process of rebalancing does not give rise to any tax consequences. Many retirement plans offer an automatic rebalancing feature. Once you set this in place, rebalancing is accomplished without further action from you. Automatic rebalancing also removes in some measure our emotional biases. During a market sell-off, not many of us are bold enough to buy more of something that has declined significantly in recent weeks. Yet, if an automatic rebalance election is triggered at that time, you capitalize on the opportunity to buy more of a depressed asset which surely has less risk and a higher return potential going forward. There are typically two elections that dictate how your investment assets are allocated. The first is your instructions for how new contributions are to be allocated among various investment options. The second relates to how your current investment holdings are allocated. Generally, to keep things simple, allocate new contributions and current balances in a similar fashion.

*Contributor: Woodard Peay, CFP®*

## Tip #27: Save Small Gifts

Invest money you receive as a gift (e.g., a birthday present) as opposed to buying something that you probably can live without. The decision isn't quite as enjoyable in the short term, but you will appreciate your decision as you near retirement.

*Contributor: Maggie Elliott, CFP®*

# GENERAL

**Tip #28: Choosing the Right Financial Planner**
Financial planning can be helpful for everyone, regardless of his or her income or experience handling money. Deciding on which planner to hire is a key decision, akin to finding a physician or attorney. Since you don't want to make this decision more than once, you should make your choice very carefully. Here are the criteria I recommend you use:

- **Credentials.** Your search should begin with advisors who are Certified Financial Planner™ practitioners. To become a Certified Financial Planner (CFP®) practitioner, the advisor must pass a rigorous national exam, complete three years of relevant experience, agree to abide by a strict code of ethics, and maintain thirty hours of continuing education over rolling two-year periods.

- **Experience.** There is an old saying, "There is no substitute for experience," and in the world of personal finance, this is a very true statement. I strongly recommend that you choose a CFP® who has a minimum of five years' experience in the financial planning field. Ten years or more is even better.

- **Compensation.** When hiring a financial planner, it is important for you to understand how he or she is being compensated. There is no right or wrong method of compensation, but you must know how your financial planner is being paid so that you can review his or her recommendations in the proper perspective.

  1. <u>Fee-only.</u> A fee-only financial planner receives fees directly from the client and never receives commissions from the sale of products. A CFP® describing his or her services as "fee-only" is prohibited from receiving commissions in any client relationship at any time. If you want to work with a fee-only planner, be sure to ask the planner if they *ever* receive commissions from the sale of products. If the answer is yes, you need to keep searching. Tip: Some planners will respond, "Yes, I'm a 'fee-based' planner." This is not the same as fee-only. Typically, fee-based means that they do sell products and receive commissions but

will 'credit' the commissions received against planning fees.

2.  <u>Commission only.</u> Here the financial planner does not charge a fee for the planning work but rather receives commissions from the sale of products recommended as a result of the planning work.

3.  <u>Commission and fee.</u> Many financial planners charge a fee for developing your financial plan and then receive commissions if you buy recommended products.

There are pros and cons for each style of compensation. Decide if you have a preference, and in any case, be certain you know how your advisor is being paid (and how much).

-   **Custodian.** Be sure to understand who, or what institution, will have custody of your money. Be leery of advisors who custody assets or money with their own private company as opposed to using a third party, such as Charles Schwab (**think Bernie Madoff**). This will give you peace of mind in knowing your money is safe and secure.

-   **Chemistry.** Ideally, when you choose a professional advisor, you will be selecting someone with whom you will work with for the rest of your life. However, it is not unusual to find a competent advisor whom for some reason you do not click with. Call it a difference of personality. Most professional advisors will meet with you initially without charge. This first meeting is used to determine the scope of the work to be performed. You should also use this first meeting as an opportunity to determine whether the advisor is someone you feel you would be happy working with long-term.

To find a Certified Financial Planner™ practitioner near you, visit www.CFP.net. You can enter your zip code and refine your search using a number of alternatives including fee-only versus commission or commission and fee.

*Contributor: Stewart Welch, CFP®, AEP*

## Tip #29: Turn Dreams into Goals and Improve Your Likelihood of Success

Emmitt Smith, a Pro Football Hall of Fame running back said in his Hall of Fame acceptance speech that "a dream is only a dream until you write it down, and then it becomes a goal." Goal setting was a huge part of Emmitt Smith's career success, and a recent Harvard study supports its importance. The study, conducted with Harvard graduate students, found that ten years after the initial survey, students with goals and detailed plans to accomplish them, earned ten times more money than those who had goals but never wrote them down and those who had no goals at all. While this study focused on the positive financial impacts of goal setting, the benefits apply to all walks of life. Do yourself a favor: determine what you want out of life, and write down a detailed plan to get there!

*Contributor: Marshall Clay, CFP®*

**Tip #30: Protect Your Money**
Fraud and identity theft through hacking financial accounts is happening more and more. I recommend that you check your credit report twice a year; now and again at midyear. Your first one is free through www.annualcreditreport.com. For the midyear check, you can request all three credit reporting companies in one report for $29.95 through www.equifax.com. In addition, download smartphone apps for your credit cards and bank accounts and check them several times per week.

*Contributor: Kimberly Reynolds, MS, CFP®*

## BONUS TIP: Protect Your Credit Cards from Theft

An easy way to protect yourself from someone using your credit card without your permission is to set up "Alerts" through the credit-card company's website. I set mine so that anytime there is a charge of $20 or more, I immediately receive a text that states the amount and company name where the charge was made. There's a lot of comfort when I get a text 'ping' as I exit the grocery store showing the charge I just made.

*Contributor: Stewart Welch III, AEP, CFP®*

## Tip #31: Track Your Spending for Thirty Days

People always tell me they don't have money left over for savings. To that I say, "Right!" I have never met a person or couple who isn't wasting a lot of money by spending impulsively that a week later they can't even recall! Try this experiment: buy an inexpensive small notebook and write down every penny you spend for thirty days; then evaluate your spending. What did you waste money on? Do you see a pattern of misspending such as eating out or buying high cost, low nutritional food items? Could you divert 10 or 20 percent to retirement savings without dramatically affecting your lifestyle? We often find substantial savings in reducing property and casualty, life, and other insurance products costs.

*Contributor: Stewart Welch III, AEP, CFP®*

## Tip #32: Give a Percentage of Income for Financial Freedom

This concept probably sounds counterintuitive at first glance, but disciplined giving can truly lead to emotional financial freedom. A few years into our marriage, my husband and I resolved to give a certain percentage of our before-tax income to our church. This was hard, but we made it work. Fast-forward a few years later, and we introduced the cost of daycare (not cheap), and giving got even harder. We updated our budget again and again to make all of the pieces fit. What we found is that we were able to focus our spending on things more closely aligned with our values and toss out some of the mindless spending we're all guilty of doing. Don't get me wrong, I love a good dinner at a nice restaurant, so this wasn't about cutting down to bare bones spending as much as identifying the things that are important to us and decluttering our expenses. This exercise helped us to know that we don't have to be tied to stuff to live according to our values, which in my mind gives us a lot of emotional freedom. Now when we get a raise, bonus, or gift, it's easier to save additional funds and not give in to the urge to blow it on things that don't matter to us.

*Contributor: Beth Moody, CFP®*

## BONUS TIP: An Easy Way to Increase Your Retirement Savings

Say you can't afford to increase your retirement savings? Try this: Every time you get a raise, commit one-half of it to your retirement savings (i.e., increase your 401(k) contribution). Do the same thing when you get a bonus. You'll increase your lifestyle and be surprised at how effortlessly you dramatically impact your long-term retirement savings.

*Contributor: Stewart Welch III, AEP, CFP®*

## Tip #33: Serve Your Country and Reap the Benefits

For over seven and half years I served as an officer in the US Army. From the opportunity to train with and learn from the greatest leaders in the world, to the ability to challenge myself in the most extreme circumstances, to the bonds and friendships I forged, to the amazing help I received with the financing of my undergraduate- and graduate-level educations, the rewards I received from this experience were immeasurable, and I would not exchange them for anything. As I look back on my military experience I am amazed that more American citizens do not take advantage of this opportunity. If you are a young American, there is no way to get your adult life off to a better start. Serve your country, grow, and reap the benefits of this great experience, and it will set the tone for the rest of your life.

*Contributor: Marshall Clay, CFP®*

## Tip #34: Monitor Subscriptions

Be aware of the monthly and yearly subscriptions that you have auto drafted from your bank accounts. Recently I went through all the subscriptions I was paying for and canceled each one that I felt like I could live without. In the end, I canceled three or four subscriptions, which is going to save me around $500 this year. Some common examples include TV streaming, music streaming, and grocery/meal delivery services. When you cancel an auto draft expense, immediately transfer that monthly expense to an auto-investment in either a personal investment account or retirement account (up your 401(k)). Ten dollars a month doesn't sound like much, but you could be spending hundreds each year without realizing it.

*Contributor: Maggie Elliott, MS, CFP®*

## Tip #35: Shop Around Online

Shopping online has saved us money. My husband and I are updating our kitchen and have been able to buy items online for significant savings. Purchasing the kitchen cabinet hardware online cut the cost almost in half. The lighting was over $300 cheaper online. To make matters better, shipping is usually free when you shop online. Number-one online retailer: www.Amazon.com.

*Contributor: Ramona Boehm*

## BONUS TIP: Amazon Prime

Is Amazon Prime worth the money? For an annual fee (currently $100), you get free shipping on most Amazon purchases, and you get Amazon Video (similar to Netflix) included for free plus many other benefits. You might just be willing to drop your cable TV subscription (and save some serious money). Amazon Prime is so easy to use—they may take over the world!

*Contributor: Stewart Welch III, AEP, CFP®*

## Tip #36: Savings Apps

Here's a trick for saving money at the grocery store. Household items have become increasingly more expensive as the years go by, and if you have a household of teenagers in the home, your grocery budget implodes every month! I have recently started using multiple websites in order to save money everywhere I go and shop. If Walmart is your thing, then I suggest the Walmart Savings Catcher app. I have downloaded the app to my phone, and as soon as I complete my shopping list, I am able to scan my receipt to the app and "Savings Catcher" goes out onto the web to search for sale items at a lower cost with competitors, than what I paid. If I bought a bag of potatoes, let's say for $4.59 at Walmart, but savings catcher sees this item on sale with a competitor for $3.99, I will receive a total of the difference in savings of $0.60 to my Savings Catcher Account. Believe it or not, it adds up quickly. I have saved a total of $6.68 all at one shopping trip with the Walmart app. Just recently I used my accrued savings by transferring over to a Walmart e-card. I had let my savings stack up to where I had $38.45 on my card that I used for future purchases! It's free money to use when you want!

*Contributor: Wendy Weber*

## Tip #37: Savings Apps (continued)

My daughter, who is in college, is always trying to save a buck! She told me about this website called Ibotta. This is another site you can download to your phone from the app store. Same concept as above, however you get to see the sale items before you go! Ibotta shows the stores you wish to shop in and by clicking on the store, it will bring up all sale items for the week/day! You click on the items you would normally purchase, unlocking items you are going to purchase on your grocery list. By clicking on the items and "unlocking" the savings this will add those items to your unlocked coupons. Once you finish shopping you just scan your receipt, and the savings for each item unlocked will be applied and deposited to your Ibotta App Account. It's that Easy! With hundreds of stores on the app, you can save a ton of money wherever you go and shop, and it's no longer necessary to clip and take coupons with you anymore. If you are like me, I would clip them and just store them in my wallet, I would forget to ever redeem them and then have to throw them out once expired! Also with this app if you create a group/team with your friends and relatives and get them to also use the app, you receive bonuses on your account! Sign up a friend/relative to your team and receive a ten-dollar bonus immediately to your account—what a deal!

*Contributor: Wendy Weber*

## Tip #38: How to Negotiate Your Cable Bill

When I signed up for new cable service a year ago, I received a great twelve-month promotional rate for Internet and cable that included all of the premium channels. Knowing that the price would increase substantially in one year, I planned to drop the premium channels at that point. When it came time to start dropping channels, I tried to call but wound up talking circles with somebody until I finally hung up.

I tried the online chat option which is great because you can print the transcript and don't have to worry about a language barrier. I simply told them that my rate was too high and asked how much I could save by dropping the premium channels. Rather than dropping channels, they offered to lower my rate to twelve dollars per month more than my original promotional rate, increase my internet speed by 30 percent, and send me a free tablet with 2 GB of data for only a forty-five-dollar activation fee. After telling them I did not want the tablet, they offered the same deal with no activation fee.

Thirty minutes on online chat got me almost all the way back to what I was paying, faster Internet, and a free tablet. These companies do not want to lose your business, so it can certainly pay off to haggle. The worst that can happen is they tell you no.

*Contributor: Foster Hyde, CFP®, CFA*

## Tip #39: Adopt the MVP Approach to Investing

It is easy to think of managing money and investing for your future as a complicated endeavor, but it is really quite simple. By following the MVP approach, whether you work with a financial advisor or not, you will set yourself up for success in the short-, near-, and long-term. The MVP approach is as follows:

<u>**M**anage risk</u>
- Understand the amount of risk from an asset-allocation standpoint to meet your stated goals (see tip #1).
- Understand the risk you are actually taking, and make the necessary adjustments.

<u>Constantly seek **V**alue</u>
- Consistently monitor your securities in all assets classes.
- Rebalance your portfolio, at least annually, to book profits in appreciating assets, and redeploy those profits in a way that helps keep your risk at appropriate levels and allows you to take advantage of securities offering better value.

<u>Patience above All</u>
- Develop a strategy you believe in, and stick to it. If you are unable to develop a sound strategy on your own, hire a financial advisor to help. Whatever strategy you choose to adopt, make sure that it is easily understood in terms of how it helps to achieve your short-, near-, and long-term goals.
- When emotion drives your investment decision, the result is too often a bad investment result.

*Contributor: Marshall Clay, CFP®*

## Tip #40: Ditch Cable
Instead of paying for your cable television subscription, try using different streaming services such as Hulu, Netflix, HBO Now, Amazon Video, or more. More times than not, you will find your demand for programming will remain unchanged and you will have saved a lot money in the process!

*Contributor: Andrea Messick*

## Tip #41: Update Your Financial Statement Annually
Every January, my husband and I update our financial statement. This is a document that lists all of our assets

(bank accounts, house, etc.) and liabilities (mortgage, car loans, etc.). While the act in itself isn't saving us money, it helps us in two ways. First, we know where we stand. That helps us identify what we need to do to achieve retirement and other financial goals. We can see if we are on track or if we need to make changes. Second, it's encouraging to see progress over time. For a sample Asset/Liability form, visit the Resource Center at www. WelchGroup.com; click on LINKS and then on ASSET/ LIABILITY REVIEW.

*Contributor: Beth Moody, CFP®*

## Tip #42: Never Stop Learning

In working with over 150 client families, one of the major psychological roadblocks many new retirees face is "What do I do now?" One piece of advice is to never stop learning. While the brain is scientifically classified as an organ, it responds to stimulation just like a muscle. So, in retirement do not send yourself out to pasture like a racehorse long past its glory days, but find things that interest you and learn about them. One option a client recently informed me of is a learning program specifically designed for mature adults offering opportunities to learn about numerous topics of their interest. The program, which now has close to two thousand members, was created by the University of Alabama and is called the Osher Lifelong Learning Institute. To learn more about this program, visit their website at www.olli.ua.edu.

*Contributor: Marshall Clay, CFP®*

## Tip #43: Look for Savings in Person and on Your Phone

I buy gently used household items or clothing in consignment shops, salvage stores, and on different apps such as VarageSale or Poshmark (which are two of my favorite apps). If you know how a particular brand of clothing fits you then you don't have to worry about returns. Everything from A to Z can be found at your local salvage store. Many times, there is nothing wrong with an item—it could be end-of-season stock, returned items from a major department store, or opened containers. Of course, I recommend that you look it over carefully before you purchase as they typically have a no-exchange and no-refund policy.

*Contributor:* Roxie Jones

## Tip #44: Intentionally Stack Your Coupons

Shop where you can stack coupons. By that I mean use a manufacturer's coupon and a store coupon on the same item, effectively doubling up on your savings! Two places where this strategy works best are CVS and Target. To make matters even better, at Target you may even get another discount using their Cartwheel app and another 5 percent off if you use a Target Red Card.

*Contributor:* Roxie Jones

## Tip #45: Write Your Own Hallmark Card

Don't buy Hallmark cards for special events like Valentine Day, birthdays, and anniversaries. Personally, write a note. Not only will you save money, but the note will be much more meaningful than a store-bought card.

*Contributor:* Michael Wagner, CFP®, CPA

## Tip #46: Supertank Printers

Over time, people spend more money on ink cartridges than they do on their actual printer. To help cut down on these costs, I recommended checking out the newly created Supertank printers by Epson. Essentially, these are printers with a refillable ink tank (which is the first big leap in printing technology in quite some time). With traditional printers, the manufacturers typically lose money on the printer itself and make up the difference when they sell the costly ink cartridges. With these new, revolutionary printers, there is a larger up-front cost to purchase the printer, but their ink reservoirs last for longer and the ink refills are significantly cheaper. Depending upon how often you print, the savings generated by switching printers could be enormous.

*Contributor: Jeff Davenport*

## Tip #47: Give of Your Time, Not Just Your Money

While charities are certainly grateful when they receive monetary donations, there are many other ways to be charitable. One great way is to give of your time. There are thousands of nonprofit organizations and charities around the world desperately in need of volunteers to help accomplish their missions. While cold hard cash is always appreciated, sometimes your time is the most valuable gift of all!

*Contributor: Marshall Clay, CFP®*

## Tip #48: Thrift Stores

Going to the thrift store is a weekly event for me. Not only do I look over furniture that I can redo, but I usually shop around for books too! Almost every piece of furniture in my house was a fixer-upper, which is something that I have gotten secondhand at a thrift store and redone to fit my style. Since I'm an avid reader, spending ninety-nine cents on a book in lieu of the twenty- to thirty-dollar price at the larger book retailers goes a long way in reaching my savings goals.

*Contributor: Kelly DeRoy*

## Tip #49: Don't Be Afraid to Fail

One of the main reasons people never achieve the type of success they would like in life is because of fear of failure. They are afraid to fail and of the short-term consequences that result. That being said, the most successful people in the world have experienced failure. So what makes them OK with failure and the rest of us so fearful of it? The answer is that they see opportunities for growth in failure and not the negative consequences most of us do. Cory Richards, a National Geographic photo journalist, summed up the appropriate attitude when dealing with likely failure before his last attempt to climb Mount Everest with no oxygen assistance. He said, "To try and fail is every bit as valuable as success as long as you push your own limits and thus gain knowledge." Cory knew that by giving it everything he had in his attempt, at a minimum he would gain knowledge about his own limits and be a better person when presented with the same challenges in the future. Do not fear failure, but embrace it, and find yourself able to climb mountains you never thought possible. By the way, Cory was successful in his no-oxygen-assistance climb to the top of Everest, becoming one of less than two hundred people in the world to do so!

*Contributor: Marshall Clay, CFP®*

# ESTATE PLANNING

**Tip #50: Review Your Will**

Do you have a will? If your answer is, "Yes, of course I do!" my next question is, "Is your will up-to-date, and are you certain what it says?"

Let's deal with the first question by assuming you don't have a will. As an example, in Alabama (intestate laws vary by state), any assets that don't pass at your death by either title or beneficiary designation will pass as follows:

- Married, no children or parents living: If it's just you and your spouse, 100 percent goes outright to your spouse.
- Married, no children, one or both parents living: Here, your spouse will receive the first $100,000 of assets plus one-half of the balance. The remainder goes to the surviving parent(s).
- Married with children: If you have children, the state dictates that the first $50,000 goes to the

surviving spouse plus one-half of the remainder. The balance goes outright to the children. Note that if the children are minors, they cannot receive property outright, and, generally, the probate court judge will appoint someone as the conservator (something like a financial custodian) to oversee the money for the benefit of the child or children. While you may assume your surviving spouse would manage the money for your children, there is no assurance of this, since it's up to the court's discretion. Don't forget—the conservator gets paid from your assets.

- Unmarried, no children but one or more parents living. If you are not married and have no children, then 100 percent of your probate estate will go to your parents equally.

- Unmarried, with children. If you are unmarried and have children, then 100 percent of your probate estate will pass equally to your living children. Note that if any of them are minors, the same rules regarding the legal conservator apply.

- Unmarried, without children or surviving parents. In this case, your probate assets will go to your siblings, equally.

Under my second question, if you do have a will, take a moment to review it in light of the current value of your estate including your home and other real estate, life insurance, retirement, and other investment plans along with personal property. If you're married, your assets likely go to your spouse, but think for a moment about the next level of heirs. If it's your children, are they capable of handling the amount of money they will receive? If not, consider the value of using a trust.

Having a valid will is very important for every adult. Intestate laws vary by state. For a state-by-state guide, visit www.WelchGroup.com; click on "Resource Center"; then "Links"; then "Intestate Succession Laws—State by State." Your best choice is to consult with an attorney who is skilled in wills and estates.

*Contributor: Stewart Welch III, AEP, CFP®*

## Bonus Tip: Negotiating a Funeral

Here are some tips to help you avoid being drawn into an emotional bad deal should you find yourself in the hot seat of negotiating a funeral:

**Start with the lists of services**. By law, a funeral home must provide you with a full price list of services and products. This list should include a minimum of sixteen standard goods and services. With this list in hand, you can better get a 'big picture' of what you want the service to look like and you can decide how much you want to spend on products such as caskets, vaults, head-stones, etc. Note that you may be able to negotiate lower prices.

**The best advice is to plan ahead.** While everyone is alive and thinking straight, why not go ahead and make those tough decisions? Again, you'll want to start with a price list which you can use as a guide to service/product choices. We ask all of our clients to complete a "Funeral Planning" form. To get your copy visit Welchgroup.com; click on RESOURCE CENTER; then LINKS; then Funeral Planning.

*Contributor: Stewart Welch III, AEP, CFP®*

## Tip #51: Give Someone the Power

A power of attorney is one of the most basic documents of an estate plan. It allows a person you appoint as your agent to act on your behalf if you were to become incompetent due to an illness or accident. If you don't have this and were to become incompetent through an accident or illness, someone would have to hire an attorney; go to court; and get a court-ordered/appointed agent to oversee your financial affairs. This agent would have to periodically report back to the court and account for every dollar spent on your behalf. As you might imagine, this can be very time-consuming and expensive.

*Contributor: Stewart Welch III, AEP, CFP®*

## Tip #52: Check Your Beneficiary Designations

While many of your assets may pass under your will or trust, some do not. Items such as life-insurance proceeds and retirement plans instead pass by way of beneficiary designation. Since these types of assets oftentimes account for a large part of people's estates, it's incredibly important to keep your beneficiary designations updated to ensure that they are properly coordinated with your other estate-planning documents and effectively carry out your wishes. Failure to do so might result in an unintended recipient, such as an ex-spouse or an irresponsible child, inheriting a sizable portion of your estate! There is also a possibility that you may inadvertently disinherit someone by omitting to update a previously completed beneficiary designation form.

*Contributor: Brett Norris*

## Tip #53: Titling Assets

Similar to incorrect beneficiary designations, erroneous titling of assets can yield unintentionally poor results without proper planning. Jointly titled property automatically transfers to the surviving owner after the death of the first owner, typically bypassing probate entirely. For that reason, it's important to take into account any interest in jointly held property a beneficiary may have when crafting an estate plan.

For example, let's assume Tom has two adult children, Alex and Sarah. Tom's entire family enjoys a beach house that is owned outright and titled jointly between Tom and his daughter, Sarah. Tom intends for his estate to be split into equal shares at his death and pass evenly to his two children. His will is written to follow his wishes exactly; however, Tom fails to account for Sarah being a joint tenant in the beach house. When Tom dies, both Alex and Sarah inherit their one-half share of their dad's estate—except for the beach house, which passes entirely to Sarah. In this scenario, Sarah's interest in the beach house is not offset by a specific bequest to Alex in their dad's will, thus creating an inequitable inheritance in favor of Sarah.

*Contributor: Brett Norris*

# EDUCATION PLANNING

**Tip #54: Give the Greatest Gift**

Part of 'living large' is using some of your resources to give to others. Give your grandchildren a gift that will last a lifetime—an education. My wife and I set up a 529 college savings plan for our granddaughter when she was born. While your gift is not deductible on your federal tax return, Alabama residents receive a deduction for contributions up to $10,000 into the Alabama plan if you file a joint return, a potential $500 tax savings. All investment income grows tax deferred and all qualified withdrawals are tax free. For more information visit www.CollegeCounts529.com.

*Contributor: Greg Weyandt, CPA, MPA*

**Tip #55: Know the Different Types of Student Loans**

Whether you are getting ready to help send a child to college, or you yourself are getting ready to go, navigating the plethora of financing options can be overwhelming to say the least. While there are a multitude of student loan options out there, not all are made equal. Depending upon which you choose, your financial future could vary greatly.

First, there are federal loans available through the Federal Direct Loan Program. Applying for these is free—all you have to do is complete a FAFSA (Free Application for Federal Student Aid) form. Under the umbrella of federal loans, there are a few different types of loans: direct subsidized, direct unsubsidized, and direct PLUS loans. Direct subsidized loans are the most favorable of the bunch because interest capitalization and accumulation is deferred while the borrower is in school. However, they are only granted to students who have a demonstrated financial need. Next are direct unsubsidized loans. These are loans that are not based on any type of financial need. Typically, they are used only after a borrower has extinguished all of their subsidized options due to the fact that they accrue interest while the borrower is still enrolled in school. Lastly in our triad of federal loans is the PLUS loan. The PLUS loan is similar to the unsubsidized loan, except it is taken out in the parent's name instead of the student. These loans accumulate interest while the student is in school, which the parent will be responsible to pay back.

Second, there are private student loans. These loans are provided by banks and other financial institutions. Similar to other loans obtained through the financial system, these private student loans are credit based—meaning that the interest rate you receive may vary depending on your creditworthiness. Usually these types of loans are taken out by a student with a credit-worthy cosigner.

*Contributor: Brett Norris*

## Tip #56: Look for Scholarship Money That's Not in Your Line of Vision

Everyone knows the common places to look for scholarship funds. College websites are a big help in showing what the university has to offer. But there are others that are not in your line of vision and have available money ready to be offered to the right high-school graduate. Here are some I had success with in my home state of Alabama. See if similar options are available in your home state as well:

- High-school websites: Counselors will list multiple scholarships available.
- Kiwanis Clubs, Rotary Clubs, women's clubs, local city organizations: All offer scholarships

to local high-school seniors. Check your local organizations.

- Distinguished Young Women (DYW) Scholarship Program (formerly Jr. Miss): The enrollment is for female high-school juniors—before their senior year. Multiple scholarships are offered to local county representatives and state and national winners. Not to mention, there are millions of scholarship funds awarded from the colleges themselves, just for being a DYW participant. (My daughter won $8,000 total for being a local county winner.) This is a great experience for your daughter, even if she doesn't win.

- SunTrust Scholarship Sweepstakes: This is a bimonthly sweepstakes drawing that you must keep on your calendar to enter religiously. Drawings begin around September and go through May. You must be proactive and reenter every two weeks for this drawing. But hey, if you win, it's $1,000 in your student's college account!

    Website: suntrusteducation.com/scholarships weepstakes.

- Restaurants and corporate companies: Many offer scholarships for your high-school senior. Wendy's Restaurant offers one each year, as well as Dr. Pepper, and so forth. Hit the websites, and check out what they have to offer!

- Your electric co-op: It will have yearly scholarships for students within their co-op area. Call or hit the website to see what your local co-op has to award. Ours offers $1,000.

- State electric co-op: This is for all Alabama senior students who apply across the state. Not related to the above, which is on the local level, so you can apply to both. This should also be listed on your local electric co-op website, or call them for information.

- College-Counts scholarship: Through the Alabama Department of Treasury. This little winner has awards of $4,000 for four-year college enrollees and $2,000 for two-year college enrollees. This is a one-time award! Website: treasury.alabama.gov/collegecounts-scholarship.

- AHSAA offers the Bryant-Jordan Scholarship Program: Students must be recommended for this scholarship by their school administration. This is for Alabama students in order to recognize them for academic and athletic excellence. Students may win on regional levels as well as state levels. Great opportunity for kids that go that extra mile. A total of approximately ninety-six regional winners and two state winners are selected each year.

Money is out there if you are willing to do the research and do the necessary work.

*Contributor: Wendy Weber*

# HEALTH AND FOOD

**Tip #57: Invest in a Better You**

Invest in yourself by getting in shape. Regular exercise has been shown to reduce stress, make you more productive at work, reduce sick days, and improve self-esteem. Plus, you might meet your next client, referral source, or employer while working out. Accountability is the key to success. Find a friend who has similar goals, and commit to work out together as "accountability partners." You'll be more likely to reach your goal and develop a special bond with your workout partner as this person reaches his or her goal too.

*Contributor: Michael Wagner, CPA, CFP*.

**Tip #58: Make Meal Planning Easy**

One of my biggest struggles early in our marriage was making meal plans each week. I love reading recipes and can browse the Internet for hours looking for meal ideas (which is funny, because I'm not a great cook). I've gotten ambitious on several occasions and ended up buying expensive ingredients that I only used once or twice before they got old. Many meals ended up costing a good bit more than if we went out to a restaurant. That's fine every once in a while, but I've found that keeping a list of easy go-to meals handy saves us money each month—the simpler the meal, the better for my wallet (and my health most of the time). This isn't complicated, but with information overload, it's easy to forget just how good (and easy) grilled chicken, steamed broccoli, and a potato can be. If you do want to try an advanced recipe with a lot of ingredients, plan ahead to see how you can use the ingredients in other meals for the week.

*Contributor: Beth Moody, CFP®*

### Tip #59: Plant a Garden

Not only is it cheaper than going to the grocery store—your veggies will be fresher and taste better. Plus you get a sense of accomplishment of growing your own food.

*Contributor: Michael Wagner, CFP®, CPA*

## Tip #60: Repurpose Empty Bottles

If you are a gardener, reuse and repurpose your empty plastic bottles to start seedlings or make watering capsules.

*Contributor: Andrea Messick*

## Tip #61: eMeals

Joining a meal plan like eMeals is a great way to save money. I caught a yearly subscription 50 percent off and paid just $29.99 for a year of weekly meal plans. This particular subscription allows you to choose from a variety of meal plans to suit your lifestyle. I love this because it gives me quick and easy weekly meal ideas instead of me trying to plan them. It's a great way to try out new recipes and plan ahead, which helps to eliminate the urge to stop at a fast-food restaurant to get dinner!

*Contributor: Kelly DeRoy*

## Tip #62: Eating Healthy and Cheap

Eating healthy is vitally important for your champagne retirement. Starting good habits now will lead to better health in the future (lower medical expenses), and learning how to eat delicious, healthy food when you're on a budget is a skill that will benefit you throughout your life. Think about an average week, and imagine you eat out for every meal. A basic lunch and dinner at a fast-casual restaurant like Chipotle will cost you about $10. That's a total of $140, just for one person per week. For reference, I spend about $60 a week on groceries *and* household supplies. Over time, those savings can add up to great things like a contribution to your Roth IRA or a fabulous trip. Planning is the most important element of sticking to your meal plan and budget. Think about what your schedule looks like for the week ahead. Do you have any lunches or dinners that will be provided? Any dinner plans with friends? Plan your prep around your schedule to avoid waste, and only make what you'll need. Nothing annoys me more than cooking food that I never have time to eat. I also don't buy all my food at one store—I look for the best prices on what I need and go where the savings are. Personally, I do quite a bit of shopping at Aldi (a discount grocer) for my produce and basic supplies like flour, flax seed, dried fruits, honey, olive oil, coconut oil, and so forth. Their fruits and veggies are of good quality and the prices can't be beat. If there's any place I splurge in my food budget, it's on meat. Taking a few minutes every week to scan the sale ads can work out in your favor in the long run. Does your local Publix or Whole Foods have grass-fed beef on sale? If so, buy what you need for this week, plus a bit more for the freezer. Set aside a few hours on Sunday to make meals that you'll enjoy but that are also convenient enough to bring to work and will be delicious if reheated. I personally can't stand reheated vegetables, so I work around that. Chili and soups are a favorite of mine, plus you can throw those in the Crock-Pot! I can't tell you how many times my best intentions have failed because I didn't spend my Sunday afternoon preparing my meals for the week. Make a plan for each week, make time to prep, and you'll see the savings add up!

*Contributor: Callie Jowers, CFP®*

## Tip #63: Kick Unhealthy Habits

By quitting unhealthy habits such as smoking, you'll not only get the satisfaction of becoming a better, healthier you, but you will also save a fair amount of money in the process. For example, based on our estimate, a twenty-three-year-old who gave up a pack-a-day habit and invested the money in equities could have over $1,200,000 by age sixty-five.

*Contributor: Michael Wagner, CFP®, CPA*

## Tip #64: Look for Alternatives to Pricey Gym Memberships

You want to be healthy. You're looking for ways to keep your waist trim, but you also want to trim your budget and looking at all of those trendy gyms and classes can be overwhelming. Don't fret over cutting out the gym membership, though. These days, you can find an abundance of free workouts. At the most basic level, you can go for a walk or run outside, or do push-ups and sit-ups in your basement. If you're looking for something a little more exciting, all you have to do is open your Internet browser to look for workout ideas or free videos. If you're like me and need a group to keep you motivated, look for free classes in your community. For example, in Birmingham, Alabama, Blue Cross Blue Shield of Alabama sponsors free evening group classes (ranging from yoga to dance classes) at Railroad Park from March to October.

*Contributor: Beth Moody, CFP®*

## Tip #65: Invest in a Coffeemaker

Purchase a nice coffeemaker that you enjoy. And make sure to use it! The savings generated by foregoing your five-dollar latte each day will be astounding over time.

*Contributor: Michael Wagner, CFP®, CPA*

## Tip #66: Health-Care Changes

Health-care policy is always changing. Due to this, it's incredibly important that you thoroughly review your plans each year and monitor the changes and how they might affect you. Review all carriers in your state for available plans and compare each plan's benefits and costs.

*Contributor: Kimberly Reynolds, CFP®*

## Tip #67: Know Your Needs

Finding the best plan is specific to each individual or family. Your health needs and current prescriptions are the two driving forces behind finding the best plan for you.

*Contributor: Kimberly Reynolds, CFP®*

## Tip #68: Research before You Buy

You need to get unbiased research when reviewing your Medicare plan options. You have the choice of Original Medicare or Medicare Advantage. Both can be fairly complicated and require a fair amount of research to adequately understand. The best resource to review the various plans is www.medicare.gov.

*Contributor: Kimberly Reynolds, CFP®*

## Tip #69: Finding the Value in Your Gym Membership

A year ago, I joined a CrossFit gym. If you've ever looked into CrossFit, you know it's not cheap. The average membership is two to three times as much as a monthly membership to your local YMCA (those usually run around fifty dollars per month). However, I knew this was the type of environment that would keep me committed to exercising regularly, so I made up my mind to fit it into my budget. One thing that helped me justify a more expensive gym membership was finding the value in the time I would be spending there. If I break down the cost by each class I attend, it works out to be around seven dollars per class if I work out five days a week. For those seven dollars, I get one-on-one coaching and training and a class environment that pushes me to compete and better myself each day. In my mind, bringing my lunch from home during the work week was making up for the expense of my membership. I've also spent less money on prescription medication over the last year than

I have in previous years and I'm following a healthier eating plan to fuel my body for workouts, so I'm spending less on food overall. All of this adds up to savings that more than make up for the monthly cost of my gym membership.

*Contributor: Callie Jowers, CFP®*

### Tip #70: Skip the Drive-Through

Eating out can cost you more than you realize and the bill will certainly add up over time. A ten-dollar meal each weekday will add up to around $200 per month. Stock up at the grocery store and prepare meals beforehand to avoid being tempted to eat out. Store any excess in the freezer, and enjoy quick meals throughout the week.

*Contributor: Maggie Elliott, CFP®*

### Tip #71: Medicare Review

If you are on Medicare, you must review your medical and prescription coverage each year!

*Contributor: Kimberly Reynolds, CFP®*

# CHILDREN AND CLOTHING

## Tip #72: Buy Used Baby Gear

You're anxiously awaiting your bundle of joy. Only the best will do for your little one! Before you run to the nearest baby store, consider buying used gear from friends of family. I recently bought a gently used baby swing from a friend for fifty dollars (the retail price was $180!). It turns out that my baby hated being in the swing, which of course I didn't know until after she was born. Although I bought something that basically went unused, I was relieved to know that I didn't pay full price for the item!

*Contributor: Beth Moody, CFP®*

## Tip #73: Share Expensive Baby Gear.

My in-laws and their friends seem to have new grand-children every other month. However, only a few of their children live in their hometown. The grandparents share and rotate baby gear (strollers, activity mats, and riding toys) as the grandchildren come to town. Although the children could pack a car full of gear with each visit, and the grandparents wouldn't technically have to buy anything, it makes out-of-town visits for the children easy and much less stressful with young children.

*Contributor: Beth Moody, CFP®*

## Tip #74: Donating or Selling Clothing

After a surgery in 2015 and some major lifestyle changes in 2016, I dropped five clothing sizes from a women's size fourteen to a size six. I've been either a size twelve or fourteen for most of my life, so needless to say, I didn't have anything to wear. I was faced with the issue of having closets full of clothing that no longer worked for me, but I was in great shape. I knew I needed to sell a few pieces, like my suits, to replace them with new items that fit, but I also knew I could help others by donating the majority of my unwanted clothing. I set up a station in my home to keep everything organized—one box to sell and one box to donate. For the items I decided to sell, I set up an eBay account and listed a few items at a time for sale. It was easy, didn't take much time, and I made a few dollars to restock my wardrobe. You can also take items to your local consignment shop and have them do the selling for you. For the items I donated, I kept track of everything with a free app developed by TurboTax called "ItsDeductible." This is a big help when tax season rolls around, as I already have a list of all the items I've donated to charity and can upload it to my tax return. Not only did I get to help others less fortunate than myself, but I also got to stay organized, so I could claim my deduction properly!

*Contributor: Callie Jowers, CFP®*

# ENTERTAINMENT AND TRAVEL

## Tip #75: Groupon Deals

If you are looking for adventure and are flexible in your planning, check Groupon's website (www.Groupon.com) on a regular basis to see what deals they're currently offering. They usually feature plenty of options such as travel accommodations, family activities, and spa services. I have a friend who recently had success using this tactic. She had always wanted to go hang gliding, and after being patient, she was able to find a discounted offer in Chattanooga. She and her boyfriend planned a last-minute weekend getaway for a fraction of the cost.

*Contributor: Maggie Elliott, MS, CFP®*

## Tip #76: Be Spontaneous

Look for last-minute travel deals on popular travel sites such as Kayak, Expedia, Orbitz, or Travelocity. The savings can be incredible and the spontaneity might make it even more fun and special.

*Contributor: Michael Wagner, CFP®, CPA*

## Tip #77: Airbnb

Airbnb is a fairly new concept that has become popular with travelers looking for alternative options to a standard hotel. Hosts list their houses or apartments on Airbnb and allow you to rent them out for a specified price. Most listings are less expensive than what a hotel room would cost and offer more living space. To use Airbnb, download the app and type in your destination. You'll be able to search through listings to find one that fits your needs. Some friends of mine recently took a trip and stayed in an Airbnb apartment. They had a living area and kitchen, and each had their own bedroom. Not only did staying at the apartment save them money, but they were also able to split the cost between six people.

*Contributor: Maggie Elliott, MS, CFP®*

## BONUS TIP: My Favorite Online Rental Site

As Maggie said, Airbnb is a great site for finding rentals. Another choice, and my favorite, is Vacation Rentals By

Owners **VRBO**. I've found it easy to navigate and have found several great deals.

*Contributor: Stewart Welch III, AEP, CFP®*

## Tip #78: Travel during the Off-Season

I always make an effort to plan a vacation during the less busy months. This usually works great because not only do I save money, but the crowds are typically smaller, so the whole trip ends up being more enjoyable.

*Contributor: Michael Wagner, CFP®, CPA*

## Tip #79: Booking Flights

Timing when to book a flight to get the right price can be exhausting. If you ask ten different people when to book your flight, you will likely get ten different answers. In my experience, the general rule that you need to book international flights earlier than domestic flights seems to hold true, but it is much harder to figure out what day of the week to book.

Checking prices daily is really not that time-consuming, if you do it right. My advice is to not limit yourself to one airline, and use a site like www.kayak.com that can look at multiple airlines at once. I personally prefer to book directly through the airline, but this gives you a good gauge of how prices compare among carriers and is quick to check. If you know your dates and destination, you may also set flight alerts on kayak or other similar sites that will e-mail you price changes and when they think the best time to book will be.

Also, don't be afraid to fly from a different city. By driving two hours each way to the Atlanta airport (which is a major hub) and avoiding that connecting flight, I was able to save almost 50 percent on the cost of an international flight. After diligently checking for about a month, I booked that flight when prices seemed too good to be true, and sure enough, the price has been hovering about 40 percent higher ever since. Flexibility and diligence can really pay off when booking flights.

*Contributor: Foster Hyde, CFP®, CFA*

**Tip #80: Go to the Library**
Check out books and videos from the library rather than purchase them. Over time this can prove to be a much cheaper alternative than buying them, and it can prove to be significantly more convenient.

*Contributor: Michael Wagner, CFP®, CPA*

## Tip #81: Movie Night

Instead of spending upward of fifty dollars to enjoy a movie and snacks at the theater, create your own movie night at home. Rent a movie from Redbox or iTunes for five dollars or less, and grab your favorite snacks from the pantry. Chances are you'll have more fun than you would at the theater, and you can pause the movie whenever you'd like!

*Contributor: Maggie Elliott, CFP®*

# SOCIAL SECURITY AND RETIREMENT

## Tip #82: Planning for a Successful Retirement Is Your Responsibility

Whether through your own initiative or by consulting an advisor, take time to develop an investment strategy for your retirement savings. It is crucial to put your strategy in writing so that its appropriateness can be reviewed annually as your life's circumstances evolve. Most companies stopped offering defined-benefit pension plans decades ago. With pension plans, your employer funded a plan designed to guarantee lifetime benefits in your retirement. More recently, few companies provide pension plans. Instead, they offer what are known as a defined-contribution plans: 401(k)s, 403(b)s, and SIMPLE IRAs are typical examples. Employees elect to make tax-deductible contributions from their paycheck and enjoy tax-deferred growth while assets remain in the plan. Often, the employer makes matching contributions or optional contributions when company profits are good. Without a guaranteed lifetime pension benefit, responsibility for building retirement assets lies now with the employee. While you can't control the market's performance, you can take action to provide the greatest opportunity for a successful retirement. Distributions from our company retirement plan often represent the primary means by which most of us provide for retirement income, supplemented by retirement income benefits from Social Security.

*Contributor: Woodard Peay, CFP®*


## Tip #83: Plan for the Unexpected

I've seen a lot of unfortunate things happen to retirees, most of which involve health issues. Be sure you have a plan for long-term health care by either purchasing insurance or setting aside appropriate financial resources. How much is enough? We'd estimate that out-of-pocket health-care costs during retirement could easily cost $250,000 to $300,000 or more. You'll also need a durable power of attorney designating someone to take care of financial matters should you become incompetent. And finally, you'll want an advanced health-care directive appointing someone to make health-care decisions for you if you're unable and outline the level of care you desire.

*Contributor: Stewart Welch III, CFP®, AEP*

## Tip #84: Know How Much Money You'll Need

Go to SSA.gov to get an estimate of your Social Security benefit based on when you plan to retire and add this to any monthly pensions for which you will qualify. Finally, based on what you're currently investing in your 401(k) and personal investment programs, guesstimate the total investments you'll have accumulated at your retirement date. Multiply this total by 0.04 to determine the inflation-adjusted annual income it should produce during retirement. This total added to annual Social Security and pension benefits equals your retirement income. If, as in most cases, it's not enough to support your desired retirement lifestyle, develop a plan now to reduce the gap. That could include saving more, reducing expenses, or planning to work longer (at least part time). For a quick and easy retirement calculator, visit the Resource Center at www.WelchGroup.com, click on "LINKS," and then "RETIREMENT PLANNING CALCULATOR."

*Contributor: Stewart Welch III, CFP®, AEP*

## Tip #85: Contribute Now

There is often a period before a new employee is permitted to begin participation in the company's retirement plan. However, as soon as you are eligible to become a retirement-plan participant, take full advantage. If you have recently joined the workforce, there are several bene-fits from taking action immediately. First, while younger people may have student debt to contend with, they often have fewer obligations than older employees, who are responsible for families and need to provide for education expenses and mortgage payments. Second, it's not how much money you save for retirement but to some extent, when you save it. Electing to save part of your paycheck into a retirement plan as soon as possible greatly enhances your odds of building significant wealth thirty-five to forty years later through the power of compound growth. It also establishes a critical habit of paying yourself first. Through the benefit of the tax deduction afforded by sal-ary deferred contributions, the government is effectively making a portion of the contribution for you.

*Contributor: Woodard Peay, CFP®*

## Tip #86: Disciplined Investor

Unlike your coworkers who may discontinue their contri-butions in the midst of a severe bear market, you should continue your contributions and remain invested. We have talked to countless people who confess that during the 2008–2009 bear market, they simply stopped con-tributing to their retirement plan. Others took a further step and liquidated their investment positions within their plan. Remember, while you are in the wealth accumulation portion of your financial life, you are a buyer, not a seller. To some extent, particularly if you are younger and have years until the remotest prospect for retirement, a down stock market simply presents an opportunity to buy more shares at a discounted price. The stock prices that truly count are twenty to thirty years hence. In order to be a successful investor, all of us are required to make a leap of faith, trusting that somehow the world holds together and that economic activity, no matter how volatile, continues to grow over time. There is nothing to be gained by taking a pessimistic view of the world while holding cash on the sideline. While it never feels this way at the time, those who continued to make disciplined contributions to their retirement accounts in 2008 and who remained invested were rewarded with a dramatic rebound over the next two or three years.

*Contributor: Woodard Peay, CFP®*

## Tip #87: Social Security Maximization Strategy

Tip #87: Social Security Maximization Strategy

More Americans are living longer thanks to better healthcare. To maximize Social Security benefits earned, the higher-earning spouse should delay their Social Security to age seventy. By delaying to age seventy, the higher-earning spouse's benefit rises 8 percent for each year delayed beyond normal retirement age (age sixty-six currently). If the higher-earning spouse predeceases the other spouse, then the surviving spouse steps into the deceased spouse higher Social Security benefit. Be aware of new Social Security rules put into place in 2015 that allow for spousal benefits only if the other spouse has claimed and receiving their own Social Security benefit. However, for anyone born on or before January 1, 1954, the "restricting an application for spousal benefits only" is still an allowable strategy.

An example of this strategy would be when a married couple who are the same age turns normal retirement age (sixty-six), the lower-earning spouse can claim his or her own regular Social Security benefit while the higher-earning spouse continues to delay to age seventy. But the higher-earning spouse gets a spousal benefit from age sixty-six to age seventy equal to one-half of the lower-earning spouse's Social Security benefit by "restricting their application for spousal benefits only."

For example, husband and wife are both age sixty-six. Husband's age-seventy benefit is $3,050 per month. Wife's age–sixty-six benefit is $1,500 per month. Wife files at age sixty-six. Husband waits to age seventy, but while waiting he restricts his application for spousal benefit only at the same time the wife files for her age–sixty-six benefit. The husband now gets $750 per month spousal benefits while waiting for his own delayed age-seventy benefit of $3,050 per month. Family benefit while waiting for husband to turn seventy is $2,250 per month. Once the husband turns seventy, family benefit increases to $4,550 per month. To make up the income difference for waiting to age seventy for Social Security, a person can continue to work or draw money from their savings.

*Contributor: Hugh Smith, CPA, CFA, CFP®*


## Tip #88: Consider Working Longer

Consider the benefits of working past full retirement age, at least to age seventy. By working and making enough to supplement a Social Security strategy, a pre-retiree can continue to let savings grow, and by working, he or she can stay engaged. While working in older years, try and schedule your work where you can still do bucket list items—maybe these items are shorter trips to a National Park (Zion or Yosemite) where you can hike and stay in one of the historic lodges. Save longer trips to Europe or Hawaii until full retirement.

*Contributor: Hugh Smith, CPA, CFA, CFP®*


## Tip #89: Create a Social Security Account

Since the passing of the OASDI program in the 1930s under President Roosevelt, Social Security benefits have played an important role in the shaping of American society and culture, primarily in the form of retirement benefits. Each person's benefit, or lack thereof, factors heavily into his or her financial life typically by way of retirement planning. That said, it's not uncommon for a person to be lacking an understanding of the system and what benefits he or she is entitled to until the time to start planning for retirement has long since passed.

Fortunately for us, the Social Security Administration allows you to create an online account where you can review several important items such as your estimated benefits (retirement, disability, survivors, family, etc.), your earnings records, taxes paid, and how many credits you have. I recently set up my account and use the provided information to plan for the future.

Making an account is simple, all you have to do is go to www.ssa.gov, click on the "sign in/up" link, click on the "my Social Security" link, and then go to "Create an Account." After providing some personal information and answering a few security questions, you will have an account and the ability to review all of the aforementioned information.

*Contributor:* Brett Norris

## Tip #90: Enjoy Your Retirement

One of the hardest things to do after a life of wealth accumulation is to enjoy the fruits of your labor and learn to spend some of your money. For most, the very reason they were able to accumulate so much money in the first place is because they did the exact opposite and held on to every penny. While reckless spending is certainly not advised, enjoying the results of a lifetime of hard work is. The late great professional skier and BASE jumper Shane McConkey once said, "We have one life to live, so make the most of it today or else you are wasting time!" I agree with Shane and would encourage everyone to make a list of things they want to see and do before they die, and do them. You worked hard! You deserve it!

*Contributor: Marshall Clay, CFP®*

## BONUS TIP: Why Are You Holding On So Tight?

To Marshall's point, I find many people (couples) not spending during retirement because they want to leave something for their children. After observing families for more than thirty years, I have found that the next generation has no problem spending your hard-earned money, and in many cases the free money can do more harm than good. So, the next time you're thinking, "Should we spend this money on a trip for us?" go ahead and do it!

*Contributor: Stewart Welch III, AEP, CFP®*

# CREDIT CARDS

## Tip #91: Guard Your Debit Card(s)

Fraudulent credit-card charges are typically easy to handle with little or no losses to you. Debit cards are an entirely different story. If a thief uses your debit card information to purchase something or access your ATM, that money is gone from your checking account and won't be restored until your bank goes through an investigative process. This can take weeks, and you'll be out the money until it's resolved. If you have and use a debit card, guard it and your information very closely, and I recommend monitoring your account activity on a daily basis. If there is a problem, you'll want to catch it early.

*Contributor: Stewart Welch III, CFP®, AEP*

## Tip #92: Stolen Credit Cards

If someone has stolen your credit information or you suspect you are vulnerable to theft, you can place a fraud alert or credit freeze on your account. Fraud alerts are good for ninety days and then are automatically removed unless you reestablish them. This alerts any company seeking your credit file that you may be a victim of fraud, and they should take extra precautions to verify that new or additional credit requests are valid. A credit freeze is designed to prevent your credit file from being released without your expressed permission. Credit freezes are good until cancelled, and you have the option to temporarily remove the freeze if, for example, you are applying for a loan or additional credit. If you have been a victim of credit fraud, there is generally no charge for these services; otherwise a small charge may apply.

*Contributor: Stewart Welch III, CFP*®, *AEP*

## Tip #93: Maximize Credit-Card Rewards

I use my Capital One Venture card as a debit card. We charge our utility bills, cell-phone bills, home-security bill, groceries, gas, gift purchases, household items, and repairs—everything we are allowed. The key to this working is paying your credit-card bill in full when it's due. By doing this, we are able to take trips to California each year and visit family for free. When our daughters got married I used credit-card points to buy their wedding dresses. Capital One does not charge an annual fee, and there are no hidden fees. We have successfully done this for over twelve years. You do need to be disciplined and keep up with your balance. Another perk to having this card is that you can easily see where your money is going. The statement can be viewed by categories. For example, you can view how much you spent on gas or food. Capital One does the bookkeeping for you.

*Contributor: Ramona Boehm*

## Tip #94: Credit-Card Debt-Elimination Strategy

From a mathematical perspective, the most advantageous way in which to eliminate your credit-card debt is to make minimum payments on all of your card balances while directing all available cash flow to the one card with the highest interest rate. Once it's fully paid off, you continue making minimum payments on all cards except the one card that now has the highest interest rate, which you'll now focus on paying the minimum payment plus all extra cash flow available. Note that the card that you just paid off creates extra cash flow that you can now apply to the next card on your list.

While the above strategy is the best strategy from a money management perspective, the following alternative strategy can create an early feeling of success which can motivate you to continue moving forward.

Alternative strategy: make minimum monthly payments on all of your cards except for the one that has the smallest balance. By focusing extra cash flow on paying down this balance, you can often quickly get the satisfaction of eliminating one outstanding balance. With this sense of accomplishment, attack the next smallest balance similarly. As each balance is retired, everything else being the same, your capacity for making payments against your balances grows such that your progress accelerates. In this manner, you can move from a state of despair to one of taking positive action achieving near-term, tangible results.

*Contributor: Woodard Peay, CFP®*

## Tip #95: Choosing Credit Cards

Choosing a credit card from the hundreds of options out there can be a daunting task, as factors such as annual fees, signup bonuses, perks, and points and rewards redemptions can all fluctuate wildly. Note that I did not mention interest rate; I advocate always paying off your monthly balance since the rates are so high (typically, annual rates are well above 10 percent) so that this is not a factor I consider.

Before looking for a card, do a review to see approximately how much you will be putting on your credit card each month and what areas those expenses go toward.

If your expenses are relatively low and not concentrated on one area, then a card with no annual fee and cash back of 1.5–2 percent may be your best bet. If you travel frequently, a card that gives extra points for booking flights/hotels and allows better redemption of points by booking more travel may be best for you. Even a high annual fee of up to $450 could be justified if you are able to get such perks as airline credits and use of airport lounges. Other cards offer higher cash back or points for spending at department stores, grocery stores, gas stations, and so forth.

For good card comparisons, check out www.bankrate. com or www.thepointsguy.com.

*Contributor: Foster Hyde, CFP®, CFA*

## Tip #96: Check Your Credit Report for Free

Clearly, your credit report can have a fairly substantial impact on your life—particularly your financial life. Your credit report gives lenders and business a broad overview of your personal credit history. It contains pertinent information such as what type of credit you utilize, whether or not you pay your bills on time, and how long you have had credit accounts open, among other things. The information recorded in these reports is also used to generate your credit score, which is obviously another incredibly important item in your financial life. Due to the severity of any information being incorrect on my report, I prefer to monitor mine on a regular basis. Fortunately, everyone is able to get a free credit report from each of the three credit bureaus once per year.

To get your free report is pretty simple. All you have to do is go the www.annualcreditreport.com, request a free credit report, enter some personal information, answer a few security questions regarding your credit history, and voila! To effectively use this strategy to its full potential, I make sure to only order my report from one of the agencies each time, thus allowing me to review my report three times each year.

Once I obtain my report, I always make sure to either print a copy or save a PDF for future reference. I quickly glance over the information to make sure everything seems to be in order. Of course, if I were to find something I felt was inaccurate, I would report it as soon as possible to the respective bureau by filing a dispute online. By periodically monitoring my reports, I am able to catch fraud early and deal with it before it gets out of control.

*Contributor: Brett Norris*

# INSURANCE AND RISK MANAGEMENT

**Tip #97: Protect Against Becoming Uninsurable**

While most term life insurance policies allow you to convert to permanent life insurance as long as you own the policy (called guaranteed convertibility), some companies permit conversion to occur for only a limited number of years. For example, you buy a 15-year level term policy but you can only convert during the first 12 years. While we recommend only buying term coverage that allows conversion throughout the entire contract period, you should review your existing policies to make certain you're aware of your policy's conversion provision, particularly if you have had a change of health status.

*Contributor: Brett Norris*

**Tip #98: Applying Risk Matrices to Everyday Life**

One of the most commonly used tools in the world of risk evaluation and management is a relatively simple tool called a "risk matrix." In its simplest form, a risk matrix is the product of two dimensions, severity and probability. The combination of the two will allow any potential event to be assigned a place on the matrix (dependent on your assessment of said event), which will help determine the appropriate action for you to take.

With respect to the above matrix, the further away an event falls from the bottom left-hand corner, the more conscientious you should be of your approach. In the matrix that I created, an event that falls in one of the red squares should either be insured against or avoided altogether. To help explain the practical application, I'll go through a few personal examples of how I have utilized the aforementioned matrix in some of my personal risk-management decisions.

I was recently considering the possibility of my becoming disabled. Pretty quickly, I assigned the probability of this happening as possible and the severity as intense. Possible since, statistically, one out of five people will suffer a long-term disability during their career; intense since a long-term disability would mean loss of income. Since this potential event fell in a square that is pretty far away from the safe zone of the bottom left-hand corner, I decided to insure against this risk by purchasing disability insurance. Contrarily, I was asked whether or not I'd like to purchase insurance on a new cell phone I bought not too long ago. With relative ease, I assigned a spot on the matrix for the loss of the phone. I considered the severity of losing or breaking my phone as minor and the probability as possible. Due to this event falling closer to the bottom left-hand corner, I decided to not purchase the insurance.

Typically, one should only purchase insurance for the risk(s) that one cannot afford to take personally. Creating a simple matrix like the one above and applying it to everyday risk-management scenarios will help you analyze situations and make well-thought-out decisions.

*Contributor: Brett Norris*

## Tip #99: When Does It Make Sense to Purchase Individual Vision or Dental Insurance?

If you're like me and don't have company-provided vision or dental insurance, it can be hard to decide if it's worth the expense of purchasing your own policy. In many cases, it makes more sense to deposit what you would pay in premiums into a savings account to cover any necessary vision or dental expenses. However, if you take time to run the numbers, you can sometimes be better off paying for an insurance policy. Personally, I wear glasses and contacts and have a higher risk for glaucoma, which means that I have to undergo a few more tests on an annual basis that aren't covered by my major medical insurance. I also enjoy being able to see and want to take good care of my vision. In total, my out-of-pocket costs without insurance coverage for a normal year when I'm only getting routine tests and a year's supply of contacts runs about $1,100. A vision-insurance policy that pays for my exam plus $230 toward contacts means I spend $323 out-of-pocket for all those services and a year's supply of contacts. In total, I pay $324 per year in premiums for this policy. With the insurance, my out-of-pocket cost is $647. This saves me about $453 per year. The savings go up significantly if I have to have new glasses (this happens every four or five years). Last year, it was time to get glasses. My total cost for glasses, contacts, eye exam tests, and so forth, would have been more than $2,500 without insurance. I only paid $700 out-of-pocket plus $324 in premiums, saving me over $1,500.

The same goes for privately owned dental insurance. I have old amalgam fillings that will need to be replaced over the next couple of years. Without insurance, each of these replacements is about $150. My dental insurance premium is $252 per year and covers my biannual exams and x-rays with a $50 copay and will pay for 80 percent of all routine dental services (all those replacement fillings).

An example of a year in which the policy makes sense is below:

| Service | Cost with Insurance | Cost without Insurance |
|---|---|---|
| Biannual Cleaning and Exam with X-Rays | $50 | $140 |
| 5 Amalgam Filling Replacements | $150 | $750 |
| Policy Premiums | $252 | 0 |
| Total Out-of-Pocket Cost | $452 | $890 |

Using the example above, we can see that the out-of-pocket cost to me is $438 less with the dental insurance plan than if I paid everything out-of-pocket. It may not make sense for me to continue to hold the policy once I finish replacing the fillings I have, and at that point, the dollars I'm spending on premiums will be directed to my personal savings account. Take some time and evaluate your out-of-pocket dental- and vision-care expenses and see what's best for you.

*Contributor: Callie Jowers, CFP®*

## Tip #100: What to Do with Your Term Life Insurance

Term life insurance is an important tool in the financial planning toolbox. As a financial advisor, one of the most often asked questions I'm asked about life insurance is, "Do I still need my life insurance?" My answer is as varied as the people who ask the question. It wasn't so long ago that life insurance was needed to pay death taxes for a lot of families, but when Congress increased the death-tax exemption to $5 million per person, suddenly that reason disappeared for all but the top 1 percent of families in America. Now, the primary reason for owning life insurance is to provide financial protection for a surviving family should a primary earner die prematurely.

If the reason you are purchasing life insurance is to protect your family should you die prematurely, term insurance is typically your best choice since it lasts for a specific period, typically ten, fifteen, twenty, or thirty years. This makes it easy to match up a life-insurance policy for, say, a twenty-year period when you are raising a family. Once the kids have graduated and are on their own, the insurance is no longer needed. Or you use a thirty-year term policy to give you time to save for retirement through your 401(k) plan and personal investment plan.

When we are deciding whether to keep or drop a life-insurance policy, we generally look at three factors:

1.  Is the need still there? If the kids are grown and on their own; if you've saved enough money for retirement; if you no longer have dependents; then the insurance may have fully served its purpose and can be dropped.

2.  Future liquidity required? The $5 million death-tax exemption per person has now risen to $5,490,000 due to cost-of-living increases. For a married couple, that means your estate can be nearly $11 million before you'll owe death taxes. Clearly this is not an issue for most families, but it does need to be reviewed being sure to include

the proceeds of any life insurance plus possible inheritances.

3. How's your health? Let's assume for a moment that the answers to numbers one and two above suggest that the insurance could be dropped. We also want to check the health of the person insured. We have a number of clients who no longer need their life insurance but whose health has deteriorated to the point that they have become totally uninsurable. In other words, they purchased the life insurance when they were in excellent health (and therefore got excellent rates), but now they couldn't buy it at all. Crudely put, the life insurance has become a good investment.

Recommendation: If you have term life insurance and are asking yourself the question, "Should I keep my policy?" have your financial advisor review your policy and your facts to help you determine the best course of action.

*Contributor: Stewart Welch III, CFP®, AEP*

# Meet the Contributors

**Stewart Welch III, AEP, CFP®**
*Founder and Managing Member*

Stewart H. Welch III founded his company in 1984 and is the managing member of The Welch Group, which specializes in providing *fee-only* Wealth Management services to affluent health-care professionals and retirees throughout the United States.

*Money, Worth* and *Mutual Funds* magazines named him as one of the top financial advisors in the United States. *Medical Economics* named him as one of the 2012 and 2013 top financial advisors for doctors, and in 2014, *Dental Practice Management* magazine named him as one of the top financial advisors for dentists. In addition, *Bloomberg Wealth Manager* has named The Welch Group one of the 150 top wealth-management firms in the country.

Mr. Welch has coauthored four books: *The Complete Idiot's Guide to Getting Rich* (Alpha Books, NY, NY), *J.K. Lasser's New Rules for Estate and Tax Planning* (John Wiley & Sons, Inc., NY, NY), *J.K. Lasser's Estate Planning for Baby Boomers and Retirees* (Macmillan, USA), *10 Minute Guide to Personal Finances for Newlyweds* (Macmillan/ Spectrum), and *THINK Like a Self-Made Millionaire* (Morgan James Publishing). In addition, Mr. Welch is a financial columnist for the *AL.com,* the largest media outlet in Alabama. He has also appeared on various TV and radio shows including CNN (NY), Fox News Network (NY), and CNBC (NJ) and is often quoted in national press including the *Wall Street Journal, Fortune, Money* and TheStreet.com.

A Certified Financial Planner™ practitioner since 1983, Mr. Welch is a past member of the board of directors for the Certified Financial Planner Board of Standards Inc. He also has served on the Charles Schwab & Co., Inc. Institutional Advisory Board and as president of the Birmingham Estate Planning Council.

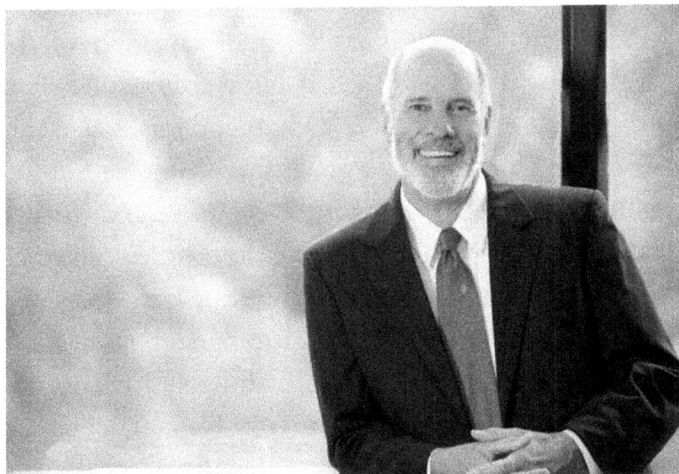

**Greg Weyandt, CPA**
*Member and Director of Operations*

Greg Weyandt joined The Welch Group in 2001 and has more than forty years of business experience in the financial-services and health-care arenas. Greg received his bachelor of arts from Auburn University in 1973 and his master of professional accountancy from Georgia State University in 1977. He is a member and Director of Operations and Chief Compliance Officer, and he also sits on the Investment Committee. Greg's professional experience includes more than eight years with the Birmingham office of PricewaterhouseCoopers, after which he served as the Chief Financial Officer of a private health-care company. Before joining The Welch Group, he served on the executive team at Brookwood

Medical Center. Greg is a CPA and a member of the Alabama Society of Certified Public Accountants. He is on the board of the Hoover YMCA and serves as chairman of the board of directors of the YMCA of Greater Birmingham. He also sits on the executive and finance committee as well. Greg is also on the board of Silverock Cove Homeowners Association where he is the treasurer. Greg is also a member of the Birmingham Track Club and is a recent convert to paddle boarding. Other outside activities include spending time with his grandchildren, working in his yard, following Auburn football, and spending time between the beach and the lake.

**Hugh Smith, CPA, CFP®, CFA**
*Member and Chief Investment Officer*

Hugh Smith brings more than twenty-seven years of business experience to The Welch Group. Hugh is member of the firm and serves as Chief Investment Officer. He is also the Chairman of the Investment Committee. He specializes in the area of equity and fixed income investment research, portfolio management, and income-tax planning. Hugh developed the analysis tools the firm uses to perform its wealth-management services, including the firm's proprietary wealth-management index. Hugh also partnered with the founder and the Investment Committee to develop the firm's proprietary dividend stock portfolio, tactical investment strategy, and fundamental index equity portfolio.

Before joining The Welch Group, Hugh was the Chief Financial Officer and part owner of a closely held business for five years. Before that, he worked in the Birmingham office of Arthur Andersen for nine years. Hugh received his degree in accounting from the University of Alabama in 1987.

Hugh has been quoted in top financial periodicals such as *Kiplinger's Personal Finance, Wall Street Journal,* and *Money* magazine, and has appeared on local Fox 6 News. In 2012, 2013, 2014, and 2015, *Medical Economics* named him as one of the top financial advisors for doctors.

Hugh holds the Certified Financial Planner™ certification, is a CPA (Certified Public Accountant), and CFA® charterholder (Chartered Financial Analyst®). He is a member of the CFA Institute, the CFA Society of Alabama, the American Institute of Certified Public Accountants, the North Alabama Chapter of the Financial Planning Association, and the Birmingham Estate Planning Council. Hugh is an Eagle Scout and serves on the Troop Committee for BSA Troop 28.

When not working or reading financial news, Hugh enjoys time with his family and outdoor activities.

**Woodard Peay, CFP®**
*Member and Senior Advisor*

Woodard Peay joined The Welch Group in 2003 and was named a member of Welch Investments in 2012. He has more than fifteen years of experience in the financial-services industry dealing directly with individuals and families in order to help them achieve their financial goals. Earlier in his career, Woodard worked for seventeen years in the natural gas pipeline and energy marketing industries. He graduated from Vanderbilt University with a BE in civil engineering and an MBA from the University of Alabama. Woodard holds the Certified Financial Planner™ certification.

He is a lifelong resident of Birmingham and is an active member of the Birmingham Sunrise Rotary Club. In his spare time, Woodard enjoys fresh and saltwater fishing.

**Kimberly Reynolds, CFP®**
*Member and Senior Advisor*

Kimberly is a member and senior advisor at The Welch Group. She joined the firm after graduating from the University of Alabama in 2004 with a master's degree in Family Financial Planning and Counseling. Kimberly holds the Certified Financial Planner™ certification. She is a member and a past president of the Financial Planning Association of North Alabama. She currently serves on the board of the Financial Education Outreach organization. She is also a member of the Estate Planning Council of Birmingham.

Kimberly was named a recipient of the 2011 Jack Davis Professional Achievement Award recognizing professional accomplishments in one of several fields of the Human Environmental Sciences College at the University of Alabama.

Kimberly served as an adjunct instructor for the University of Alabama and taught Income Tax Planning and Management for five years.

Kimberly is married and has two boys. She loves spending time with her family and friends.

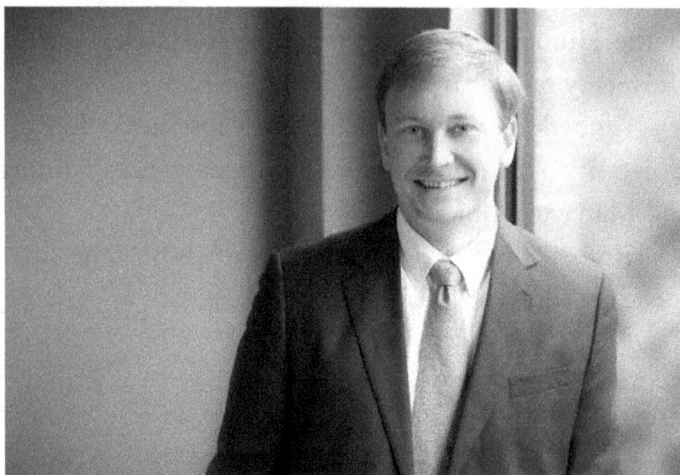

**Michael Wagner, CPA, CFP®**
*Member and Senior Advisor*

Michael Wagner has more than fifteen years of business experience in the accounting and financial fields. Michael earned his bachelor's degree in accounting from the University of Alabama in 2000 and his master of accountancy degree in 2001. Before joining The Welch Group, Michael worked as a Senior Consultant for a forensic accounting and valuation firm and also worked in the Assurance and Advisory practice for the Birmingham office of Ernst & Young, LLP.

Michael holds the Certified Financial Planner™ certification and is a CPA (Certified Public Accountant). He currently serves as the president of the Estate Planning Council of Birmingham and is also a member of the

Alabama Society of Certified Public Accountants, the American Institute of Certified Public Accountants, and the North Alabama Chapter of the Financial Planning Association.

**Foster Hyde, CFA, CFP®**
*Senior Advisor*

Foster Hyde joined The Welch Group in 2011 as an Associate Advisor and now serves as a Senior Advisor. Foster graduated from the University of Alabama with a bachelor's degree in finance in 2008 and a master's degree in Family Financial Planning and Counseling in 2009. Before joining The Welch Group, Foster worked as a consultant for a forensic accounting and valuation firm in Birmingham.

Foster holds both the Chartered Financial Analyst® designation and the Certified Financial Planner™ certification. He is also a member of the Estate Planning Council of Birmingham, the Alabama Council of Charitable Gift Planners, and the North Alabama Chapter of the Financial Planning Association.

Foster serves on the Junior Board of Directors for Red Mountain Park and served on a United Way Visiting Allocation Team in 2016.

In his free time, Foster enjoys rock climbing, hunting, fishing, hiking, traveling, and following Alabama football.

**Beth Moody, CFP®**
*Senior Advisor*

Beth Moody joined The Welch Group in October 2012 and now serves as a Senior Advisor. Beth graduated from the University of Alabama where she earned a Bachelor of Science degree in Consumer Sciences with a concentration in Family Financial Planning and Counseling in 2007 and a Master of Science degree in Human Environmental Sciences with a concentration in Consumer Economics in 2008. Before joining the firm, she worked with Welch Investments in Birmingham, Alabama, and also worked with a wealth-management firm in Atlanta, Georgia.

Beth is a Certified Financial Planner™ practitioner. She currently serves on the board of the Financial

Planning Association of North Alabama. Beth is a member of the Estate Planning Council of Birmingham, and she also volunteers with her church's youth group.

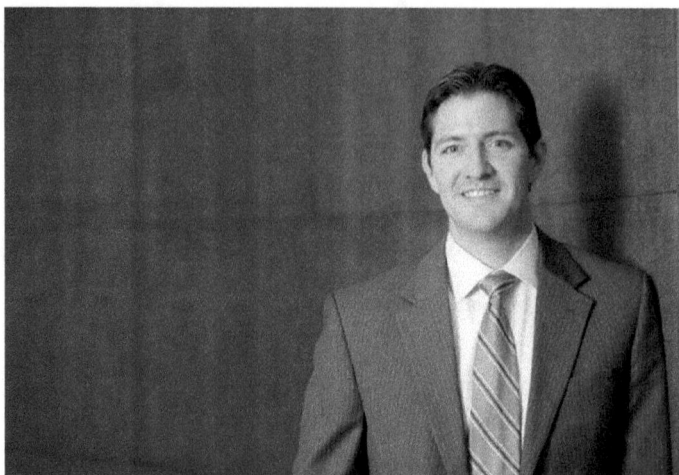

**Marshall Clay, CFP®**
*Senior Advisor*

Marshall Clay joined The Welch Group in 2012 as an Associate Advisor and now works as a Senior Advisor with Welch Investments. He is a graduate of the United States Military Academy at West Point in 2001, where he earned a Bachelor of Science degree in Human and Regional Geography and a minor in Environmental Engineering.

Upon graduation from West Point, Marshall served seven years as an Officer in the United States Army, where he performed two combat tours of duty in Iraq and one tour in the Republic of South Korea. Following his army career, he earned a law degree from Cumberland School of Law at Samford University in Birmingham, Alabama.

Marshall's passion for finance led him to pursue a career in the financial-services industry. He holds the Certified Financial Planner™ certification. His unique education and world experience greatly adds to our firm's ability to serve clients.

He is a board member of the Alabama Veterans Memorial Foundation and a member of the Kiwanis Club of Homewood-Mountain Brook, Financial Planning Association of North Alabama, and Estate Planning Association of Birmingham, Alabama.

**Callie Jowers, CFP®**
*Advisor*

Callie Jowers joined Welch Investments in 2012 as an Associate Advisor and now serves as an Advisor. She earned a Bachelor of Science degree in Consumer Sciences, with a concentration in Family Financial Planning and Counseling from the University of Alabama. Before joining our team, Callie worked as a financial planning and consumer sciences tutor for student athletes at the University of Alabama Center for Athletic Student Services.

Callie holds the Certified Financial Planner™ certification and currently serves on the board of the Financial Planning Association of North Alabama.

In her spare time, Callie enjoys spending time with her niece and nephews, working on vintage cars with her father, cooking, baking, restoring and refinishing antiques, and cheering on the Alabama football team.

**Maggie Elliott, CFP®**
*Associate Advisor*

Maggie Elliott joined The Welch Group in March of 2015 as an Investment Operations Specialist and currently is an Associate Advisor. Maggie graduated from the University of Alabama, where she earned a Bachelor of Science degree in Finance in 2012 and a Masters in Family Financial Planning and Counseling in 2013. She holds the Certified Financial Planner™ certification. Before joining The Welch Group, Maggie worked for a registered investment adviser firm in Birmingham. Maggie is a member of the Junior League of Birmingham. She enjoys traveling, reading, and spending time with her friends and family.

**Brett Norris**
*Associate Advisor*

Brett Norris joined The Welch Group in May of 2016 as an Associate Advisor following his graduation from the University of Alabama where he earned a Bachelor of Science degree in Finance. As a student, he specifically concentrated on studying personal wealth management, insurance, and risk management. Before joining the firm as an Associate Advisor, Brett spent two semesters serving internships at The Welch Group.

Brett is a member of the North Alabama Chapter of the Financial Planning Association and the Estate Planning Council of Birmingham. In his free time, he enjoys spending time outdoors, being with friends and family, and attending local music venues. Additionally, Brett is an avid fan of the University of Alabama's football team.

**Wendy Weber**
*Investment Operations Manager*

Wendy Weber joined The Welch Group in November of 2004 as a member of the Operations Department. Wendy has brought a strong customer service background and organizational skills and various professional skills that were acquired from over fifteen years of experience within the medical field in Allen, Texas.

Wendy works as a direct liaison between our advisors and Schwab. She handles the setup of new accounts and manages the balancing of client accounts and client requests on a daily basis. She also processes trades and client money transactions and works closely with our team of advisors to provide the ultimate customer service for our clients.

Wendy lives north of Birmingham near Smith Lake and loves being on the lake. She and her husband, Jason, have three daughters, Ashleigh, Katie, and Bailey, and one son-in-law, Shawn. She is thrilled to introduce an adorable new addition to the family, her first granddaughter, Carter, born May of 2014. When not at the office, Wendy enjoys spending time with her growing family.

**Andrea Messick**
*Investment Operations Specialist*

Andrea Messick joined The Welch Group in April 2013. She has almost ten years of experience in customer service and enjoys helping out everyone and everywhere she can. Andrea has quickly embraced her administrative responsibilities to the firm, as well as taking on responsibilities with The Welch Group's sister company, Welch Investments, LLC. Since joining The Welch Group, Andrea has studied the goals and inner workings of both firms and aspires to be a divergent and multifaceted member of the team.

In her spare time, Andrea enjoys trips to the Birmingham Zoo with her daughter and attending events to catch up with college friends from Jacksonville State University, where she was a member of the Marching Ballerinas with The Marching Southerners.

Kelly DeRoy, RP®
*Investment Operations Specialist*

Kelly joined Welch Investments in 2011 as an Investment Operations Specialist. Before joining the team, Kelly worked as a financial analyst for a local hospital. Kelly received her Bachelor of Science degree from the University of Montevallo in 2008 and received her Registered Paraplanner designation in 2014.

In her spare time, Kelly loves vacationing at the beach and spending time with her family. She also enjoys reading, target practice and skeet shooting, softball, and anything that allows her to tap into her creative do-it-yourself side.

Ramona Boehm
*Financial Documents Manager*

Ramona Boehm began working at The Welch Group in 2006 as the Financial Documents Manager. Ramona's goal is to provide the best service for The Welch Group clients. As Financial Documents Manager, Ramona creates and periodically updates client personal handbooks and maintains client documents. She works closely with our advisors and assists in client-related projects. Ramona represents the firm at community networking events, which she attends regularly.

In her free time, Ramona enjoys listening to music, reading, attending sports events, and spending time with family.

**Roxie Jones**
*Executive Administrative Assistant*

Roxie has been the cheerful, familiar voice of The Welch Group since 2002. Her contribution to the firm is invaluable. She is also the personal assistant to the managing member, Stewart Welch III. She helps maintain our customer database, manages mailings and packages, tracks client checks, works with office equipment vendors, keeps supplies stocked, and handles special projects as they appear. Roxie is truly a team player. She is ready and willing to do whatever it takes to get the job done.

Before joining The Welch Group, Roxie was district manager for a chain of twenty-three camera stores in the Southeast. She enjoys jewelry making and gardening in her spare time, but family and friends are her main focus.

**Jeff Davenport**
*Systems Administrator*

Jeff Davenport has more than thirty years of experi-ence in the electronics/computer industry. Before join-ing The Welch Group full time in 2001 as the Systems Administrator, he managed his own computer-support company, and The Welch Group became one of his clients in 1994. After joining the firm, he also became skilled in the back-office operations, processing trades, and maintaining the portfolio-management system for all clients.

Outside the office he enjoys family and friends, along with following Auburn football and NASCAR.